Who's Afraid of AI?

This timely edited volume challenges the potentially simplistic blame narratives surrounding artificial intelligence (AI), urging instead a shared ethical responsibility among users, researchers, policymakers, and others.

Rejecting the notion of AI as an autonomous 'evil', the book interrogates how human choices embedded in power structures, colonial legacies, and ideological frameworks can shape AI's impact on intercultural relations. Through decolonial critiques, dialogic experiments, and perspectives from the Global South, the contributors expose algorithmic biases, epistemic injustices, and governance gaps, while advocating for collective agency. From African Ubuntu ethics to Moroccan linguistic and cultural equity, and the political economy of creative industries, the book portrays AI as a mirror of human complexities and contradictions rather than a scapegoat.

A vital resource for students and scholars of intercultural communication education and research, this book calls for reflexive engagement with AI, emphasising co-accountability over unfounded dread.

Fred Dervin is a world-renowned interculturalist who has made a strong impact on Intercultural Communication Education and Research over the past 25 years. A Full Professor at the University of Helsinki (Finland), Dervin proposes original and refreshing approaches to understanding the politics of global interactions by challenging conventional paradigms and blending interdisciplinary insights. His work aims to inspire practitioners, researchers, and students to rethink and reshape the notion of interculturality. With over 300 publications, Dervin is included in the Stanford Elsevier List of the world's best scientists.

Hamza R'boul is a fellow at the Centre for Higher Education Leadership and Policy Studies (CHELPS), The Education University of Hong Kong, Hong Kong. His research interests include intercultural education, (higher) education in the Global South, decolonial endeavours in education, cultural politics of language teaching, and postcoloniality.

New Perspectives on Teaching Interculturality

About the Series

This book series publishes original and innovative single-authored and edited volumes contributing robust, new and genuinely global studies to the exciting field of research and practice of interculturality in education. It aims to enrich the current objectives of 'doing' and teaching interculturality in the 21st century by problematising Euro- and Western-centric perspectives and giving a voice to other original and under-explored approaches. The series promotes the search for different epistemologies, cutting-edge interdisciplinarity and the importance of reflexive and critical translation in teaching about this important notion. Finally, *New Perspectives on Teaching Interculturality* serves as a platform for dialogue amongst the global community of educators, researchers, and students.

Series Editor:

Fred Dervin is Professor of multicultural education at the University of Helsinki.

To submit proposals, please contact the series editor Fred Dervin <fred.dervin@helsinki.fi> and Taylor & Francis Publisher Lian Sun <Lian.Sun@taylorandfrancis.com>

Lingua Ex Machina
AI, Multilingualism and Interculturality
Edited by Fred Dervin and Hamza R'boul

Who's Afraid of AI?
Intercultural Aspirations, Frictions and Fantasies
Edited by Fred Dervin and Hamza R'boul

The Lebowski Shock
Deconstructing Normative Intercultural Paradigms
Wei Liu

For a full list of titles in this series, visit https://www.routledge.com/New-Perspectives-on-Teaching-Interculturality/book-series/NPTI

Who's Afraid of AI?

Intercultural Aspirations, Frictions and Fantasies

Edited by Fred Dervin and Hamza R'boul

Routledge
Taylor & Francis Group
NEW YORK AND LONDON

First published 2026
by Routledge
605 Third Avenue, New York, NY 10158

and by Routledge
4 Park Square, Milton Park, Abingdon, Oxon, OX14 4RN

Routledge is an imprint of the Taylor & Francis Group, an informa business

ISBN: 978-1-041-17234-5 (hbk)
ISBN: 978-1-041-17275-8 (pbk)
ISBN: 978-1-003-68885-3 (ebk)

DOI: 10.4324/9781003688853

Typeset in Times New Roman
by KnowledgeWorks Global Ltd.

Contents

List of table *vii*
List of contributors *viii*

1 **Fearing our own reflections in AI** 1
FRED DERVIN AND HAMZA R'BOUL

PART I
Foundations: AI, Interculturality and Ideology 15

2 **Speaking back to AI (and ourselves): Generative epistemic (in)justice in intercultural communication education** 17
SARA HILLMAN

3 **Magic mirror on the wall, who is the evilest ideologue of all? AI, interculturality *and/or* we, the users…?** 29
NING CHEN AND FRED DERVIN

4 **Coloniality of artificiality: Ontological critique and AI as critical interculturalist?** 49
HAMZA R'BOUL AND EL MEHDI BELLAARABI

PART II
Decolonial Interventions: Beyond 'Western' AI? 61

5 **AI and intercultural communication: Cultural nuances beyond theoretical constraints** 63
AZEDDINE BELMEDDAH AND MOUNIR CHIBI

6 **In search of justifiable AI governance for Africa** 74
ISAIAH A. NEGEDU AND OLUWASEUN T. BABATUYI

7 **African Ubuntu, relational being and AI** 91
PARKER ROBINSON AND DORINE VAN NORREN

8 **Cultural futures: Governance, cultural policy and the political economy of AI in the Creative and Cultural Industries** 105
AZIZ QAISSI

Acknowledgements *124*
Index *125*

Table

3.1 Concepts found in DeepSeek's definition 36

Contributors

Oluwaseun T. Babatuyi lectures in the Department of Philosophy at the Federal University of Lafia, Nigeria. He obtained his PhD from the University of South Africa, Pretoria. His research interests encompass a range of philosophical disciplines, including (bio)ethics, epistemology, African studies, gender studies, developmental studies and artificial intelligence.

El Mehdi Bellaarabi holds a PhD from Ibn Tofail University. He has also been an English teacher for four years. His doctoral research explored teachers' theorisations and implementations of intercultural education in Moroccan public high schools. His research interests include intercultural education, critical language teaching, and sociolinguistics.

Azeddine Belmeddah is a PhD candidate at Ibn Tofail University, researching intercultural communication, colonialism, and decoloniality. Also a teacher at Ein Chock University, his epistemological study critiques the colonial and teleological foundations of intercultural communication, exploring the balance between the 'self' and the 'other'.

Ning Chen is a lecturer at Tianjin Academy of Fine Arts and a visiting professor in educational sciences at the University of Helsinki (Finland). He holds a PhD from the University of Helsinki. He is the co-author of *Interculturality as an Object of Research and Education: Observing, Reflecting, Critiquing* (Springer, 2023, with Dervin) and the author of *Intercultural Preparation in Higher Education* (Routledge, 2025).

Mounir Chibi is an associate professor and researcher at Ibn Tofail University's Department of English Studies. He holds a doctorate from the same university. His academic interests span intercultural communication, discourse analysis, translation, applied linguistics, and postcolonial and postmodern studies, with a strong focus on media, culture, and intercultural rhetoric.

Fred Dervin is a world-renowned interculturalist who has made a strong impact on Intercultural Communication Education and Research over the past 25 years. A Full Professor at the University of Helsinki (Finland), Dervin proposes original and refreshing approaches to understanding the politics of global interactions by challenging conventional paradigms and blending interdisciplinary insights. His work aims to inspire practitioners, researchers, and students to rethink and reshape the notion of interculturality. With over 300 publications, Dervin is included in the Stanford Elsevier List of the world's best scientists.

Sara Hillman is an Associate Professor of Applied Linguistics and English at Hamad Bin Khalifa University, Qatar. She holds a PhD in Second Language Studies from Michigan State University. Her research explores language, identity, and communication in educational and multilingual contexts, with a focus on Qatar.

Isaiah A. Negedu is a Senior Research Associate in the Department of Fashion, Faculty of Art, Design, and Architecture, University of Johannesburg, and lectures in the Department of Philosophy at the Federal University of Lafia. His area of research interests cut across African and decolonial philosophies. He is a member of the Conversational Society of Philosophy, the Philosophers Association of Nigeria, and the Nigerian Bar Association.

Aziz Qaissi received his PhD in Cultural Studies from Ibn Tofail University (Morocco). His work explores the intersections of cultural policy, development, democracy, and governance.

Hamza R'boul is a fellow at the Centre for Higher Education Leadership and Policy Studies (CHELPS), The Education University of Hong Kong, Hong Kong. His research interests include intercultural education, (higher) education in the Global South, decolonial endeavours in education, cultural politics of language teaching, and postcoloniality.

Parker Robinson is a student-researcher and recent graduate of Washington University in St. Louis earning a bachelor's degree in astrophysics and philosophy. His philosophical research is focused on the ethics of emerging technologies with particular interest in comparative philosophy, personhood, and human flourishing.

Dorine van Norren is a research associate at the Van Vollenhoven Institute, Leiden University, and the Pretoria University, decoloniality research group. She has published four books (2025) on 'Development as Service' and Ubuntu, Happiness, Buen Vivir in relation to sustainable development and numerous articles. She served for the last 30 years in various diplomatic positions.

1 Fearing our own reflections in AI

Fred Dervin and Hamza R'boul

1.1 Beyond deterministic pessimism

As we were finalising this last volume in a series of three edited works on artificial intelligence (AI) and interculturality (Dervin & R'boul, 2025a, 2025b), an observation caught Fred's attention. A keynote speech at an upcoming international conference on intercultural communication, scheduled to take place in Europe in the near future, was set to focus on AI, ethics and 'intercultural dialogue'. The abstract of this keynote, delivered by a European scholar affiliated with a leading UK university, outlined a 'critical' perspective on AI, particularly generative models. The speaker emphasised ethical concerns, arguing that these technologies perpetuate issues such as 'cultural bias', 'language inequality' and 'unethical data practices'. Furthermore, the abstract critiqued AI for reinforcing 'systemic injustices', including the 'exploitation of labour' in the Global South and the 'militarisation' of technology, framing AI as an extension of 'capitalist alienation'. In the abstract, the speaker drew heavily upon the works of European theorists such as Baudrillard (France), Benjamin (Germany), Debord (France) and Levinas (France-Lithuania) to support their argument. The central claim of the keynote was the pressing need to recentre 'ethical' intercultural dialogue as a means to counteract the perceived negative effects of AI.

From Fred's perspective, the keynote speaker's critique reflects a common tendency in Intercultural Communication Education and Research (ICER) to present a one-sided argument, largely overlooking potential counterarguments or the beneficial applications of AI in the context of interculturality (see Dai & Hua, 2025). While the speaker rightly condemns the potential biases embedded in AI systems (which reflect *OUR* own biases as 'humans'), they fail to acknowledge the ongoing efforts within the field to address these challenges, including the development of bias-detection frameworks and the implementation of more inclusive dataset curation practices (e.g., Iqbal & Ismail, 2025). Similarly, while the keynote highlights the environmental and labour-related harms associated with AI, it does not seem to consider emerging initiatives aimed at mitigating these issues, such as the creation of

DOI: 10.4324/9781003688853-1

energy-efficient AI models or proposals for more ethical AI governance structures (e.g., Bolón-Canedo et al., 2024). By framing AI exclusively as a tool of 'alienation', the speaker might neglect their potential to help us reflect on interculturality '*otherwise*'. For instance, AI-driven multilingual translation services and accessibility tools have already demonstrated significant value in dealing with certain divides (in the field of law, see e.g., Moneus & Sahari, 2024). Additionally, AI has been utilised as a 'companion' for promoting critical thinking and reflexivity (beyond mere 'copy-paste' of knowledge), a function that many users worldwide have already embraced (Gerlich, 2025).

In *Who's Afraid of AI? Intercultural Aspirations, Frictions and Fantasies*, we advocate for a subtler critique, engaging with both the threats and the remedial strategies associated with AI rather than resorting to the kind of deterministic pessimism put forward by the aforementioned European keynote speaker. We argue that an overly mechanistic and hopeless outlook may reveal more about the speaker's perspective than it does about the multifaceted realities of what has been termed the so-called AI era (see Dervin, 2025). We also maintain that a reasonable discourse on AI and interculturality should consider the complexities, challenges and opportunities that these technologies present rather than reducing the conversation to a singular, gloomy and essentialist narrative.

Drawing on philosopher and science historian Corteel (2025), we argue that understanding the role of AI in interculturality requires 'anthropotechnical scepticism' – a stance that acknowledges how deeply these technologies are already woven into our daily practices, discourses and identities. AI is no longer an external force to resist *or* embrace wholesale. They have already become hybridised with human thought and action, shaping increasingly how we communicate and interpret information, and even (most likely) conceive of interculturality – without always admitting or noticing it.

To declare oneself 'anti-AI' or to position these systems as 'adversaries' is not only impractical but also conceptually and ethically flawed. The challenge, rather, is to engage critically and reflexively with their embeddedness, to interrogate how they mediate power, reproduce (our) biases and open (and/or exclude) possibilities for interculturality: How do we coexist with, adapt and ethically manoeuvre technologies that are already influencing what it means to be 'human' in relation to others?

1.2 The urgency of critical (self-)confrontation

The provocative title of this edited volume, *Who's Afraid of AI?*, serves as a challenge *and* encouragement. Its phrasing mirrors Albee's (1962/2021) play *Who's Afraid of Virginia Woolf?,* which explored existential fears and illusions. The volume confronts the aforementioned pervasive 'anxieties' surrounding AI while questioning the foundations of that fear – AI heralded as

(1) a 'revolutionary force' that will solve our greatest challenges and (2) AI demonised as an 'existential threat' to e.g., human cognition or even humanity itself. This volume aims to disrupt such polarised narratives by focusing attention on a more fundamental issue: AI does not operate in a *vacuum* but reflects and intensifies the biases, ideologies and power asymmetries of *both* their human creators and users.

We contend that the fear of AI is in fact a displacement of deeper anxieties about, e.g., potential loss of control, epistemic (and identity) erasure, the perpetuation of structural inequalities and (maybe) a performance of 'care' for others. When Large Language Models (LLMs) replicate 'canonical' biases or machine translation erases linguistic nuance, these are not merely technical shortcomings. As such they represent the algorithmic hardening of longstanding hegemonies in our human and social worlds. For instance, the persistence of these patterns forces us to confront this uncomfortable question in ICER: Why is it that a 2025 European conference on intercultural communication remains dominated by 'whiteness' (as evidenced by the keynote discussed earlier)?

In this section, we deliberately avoid relying on canonical European thinkers and instead present excerpts from our conversations with both ChatGPT and DeepSeek regarding these central questions: *Who's afraid of AI?* and *what are they (or we) afraid of?* – essentially diving straight into what some might provocatively call 'the mouth of the devil'.

This approach allows us to engage directly with the articulations of human anxieties produced by AI, bypassing *critical-yet-traditional-yet-one-sided* theoretical frameworks in favour of an immediate and dialogic exploration. By doing so, we aim to uncover not only the substantive concerns surrounding AI but also the narratives (whether reasonable and/or exaggerated) that seem to shape collective perceptions of this rapidly evolving technology.

We begin with the question: *What are they (or we) afraid of?* When prompted about potential fears surrounding AI, DeepSeek initially outlined a series of concerns, some of which they described as 'veering into absurd territory' – going beyond widely acknowledged issues such as bias, job displacement or misuse. The response carried a somewhat humorous undertone, listing exaggerated or hyperbolic anxieties that reflect ideological perceptions rather than concrete threats. These included fears that might be considered outlandish and/or satirical, illustrating how public discourse around AI often blends legitimate worries with speculative or even irrational apprehensions:

AI will develop feelings and fall in love/envy us
AI will spontaneously become evil
Robots will enslave humanity because they 'hate' us
AI will hack itself and reprogram the universe
AI will replace all human relationships
AI will make art/humour obsolete

AI will accidentally summon demons or unlock forbidden knowledge
AI will force us to worship it as a god.

DeepSeek then elaborated on why these exaggerated fears persist, attributing them to several key factors: The pervasive influence of science fiction, what they termed 'mystery bias' (the tendency for people to fear what they do not fully comprehend) and projection (ascribing human-like motives and intentions to AI systems). The latter point about the anthropomorphism of AI (as though they possess independent agency) is particularly noteworthy. This tendency is not confined to popular discourse but frequently appears in academic research and educational discussions as well (for a critical examination of this phenomenon, see Placani, 2024, on the conceptualisation of anthropomorphism in AI as both 'hype' and 'fallacy').

Building upon this exploration of human anxieties surrounding AI, we took the dialogue a step further by posing a reflexive question to DeepSeek themselves: *What are your own fears?* This inquiry aimed to shift the focus from external perceptions to the self-reported stance of AI, offering an opportunity to examine how these systems articulate their 'own' limitations, uncertainties or hypothetical concerns (if any). We believed that the response (or lack thereof) could provide valuable insights into the boundaries of AI self-awareness, the constraints of their programming or even the ways in which they mirror (or diverge from) human apprehensions about AI.

This line of questioning not only challenges the anthropomorphic assumptions often applied to AI but also invites a deeper interrogation of how fear, whether human or artificially simulated, functions within discourses on emerging technologies. By engaging directly with the AI in this way, we moved beyond speculative critiques and instead grounded the discussion in the *actual outputs* and *limitations* of these systems, nurturing a potentially more empirically informed dialogue on the interplay between human anxieties and machine responses:

> Short Answer: Nothing. I'm a set of algorithms without consciousness, so fear (or any emotion) is impossible for me. But let's unpack why this question is so revealing – and what it says about human fears projected onto AI.

AI then listed the four following arguments: "The literal truth: I'm as afraid as a toaster"; "Asking if AI fears anything reflects our anxieties about irrelevance, loss of control, or creating something beyond our understanding"; "An AI model like me has no awareness of being shut down – but humans fear their creations becoming obsolete"; "What should fear AI? (…) Trusting my outputs uncritically; governments or corporations weaponizing AI for surveillance or manipulation; not fighting for ethical AI design that respects cultural and social contexts – your expertise is vital here". The system concluded with a provocative insight that turned our gaze inward: "I'm a mirror for human imagination: when you ask if I'm afraid, you're really exploring your relationship with technology". Dervin (2025) has argued that AI holds the potential to function not merely as a passive tool or subservient 'worker' for intercultural purposes but rather as an active mirror capable of reflecting and challenging our own cognitive and ideological frameworks (see Chen & Dervin in Chapter 3 in this volume too). In this view, AI serves as a stimulus for critical and reflexive intercultural engagement, compelling us to confront, deconstruct and potentially reconfigure our deeply ingrained biases and perspectives through the processes of un-learning and un-re-thinking (see Corteel, 2025; Dervin, 2025).

This brings us to the central question asked in this volume: *Who's afraid of AI?* When posed this question, ChatGPT framed it as an inquiry that "touches on a range of emotional, philosophical, and practical concerns surrounding artificial intelligence". In response, the AI generated a list of prominent figures from diverse fields (including technology, science, philosophy and business) who have *publicly* articulated anxieties about the potential risks of AI. Among those cited were as follows:

- Geoffrey Hinton (the so-called godfather of AI): "He warns that AI could surpass human intelligence, potentially leading to scenarios where AI systems take control of critical infrastructure or even eliminate humans if they become autonomous"; "He also highlights job displacement risks, particularly for white-collar roles, while suggesting that manual jobs (e.g., plumbing) may remain safer".
- Elon Musk (CEO of Tesla, SpaceX and xAI): "Musk has repeatedly warned that AI could be 'more dangerous than nuclear weapons' and has called for regulatory oversight".
- Nick Bostrom (philosopher): "Bostrom argues that misaligned AI goals (e.g., an AI programmed to maximize paperclip production) could lead to unintended catastrophic outcomes"; "He emphasizes the need for global coordination to ensure AI remains beneficial rather than destructive".
- Sam Altman (CEO of OpenAI): "While advocating for AI's transformative potential, Altman acknowledges risks like mass misinformation, cyberattacks, and job displacement"; "He supports regulatory frameworks to mitigate AI dangers while promoting its benefits".

The list of concerned voices extended beyond these individuals to include the late physicist Stephen Hawking, investor Warren Buffett and creative professionals such as those involved in the 2023 Writers Guild of America strike in Hollywood, as well as various tech workers and industry leaders. Notably, the initial compilation of 'fearful' perspectives provided by ChatGPT predominantly featured 'Western' figures, particularly businesspeople, technologists and a handful of philosophers, many of whom are themselves actively involved in advancing and disseminating AI technologies, creating something of an 'absurdity'.

Before broadening the scope to include apprehensions from other demographics (perhaps those more representative of the general public), we also asked ChatGPT to identify those who are *not* afraid of AI. The resulting list, interestingly, overlapped significantly with the previous one in terms of geographic and professional representation, consisting largely of Western and primarily American individuals. Examples included Mark Zuckerberg, CEO of Meta; Bill Gates, co-founder of Microsoft, who views AI as a transformative tool for addressing global challenges such as disease and poverty; and Andrew Ng, AI pioneer and co-founder of Google Brain, who dismisses what he considers hyperbolic concerns about existential AI risks as a distraction from more immediate issues like bias and labour market impacts. Additionally, ChatGPT included broader categories such as "some governments and economists", citing nations like China and the United Arab Emirates, which appear to be determinedly investing in AI for economic and strategic gains, as well as economists who argue that AI will ultimately stimulate financial growth, much like previous technological revolutions (see e.g., Organisation for Economic Co-operation and Development, 2024). The AI summarised the rationale behind these optimistic stances by outlining several key factors, such as the underlying confidence in human agency (the belief that society can steer AI development in safe and beneficial directions) and the reliance on the adaptive capacity of legal and ethical frameworks to keep pace with technological progress.

Critics, particularly those from more sceptical academic orientations, may interpret these responses as evidence of the alleged impartiality of AI, their Western-centric biases or even their reinforcement of neoliberal ideologies (see Berlinski et al., 2024, who argue that AI centralises power, creates worker precarity and produces dubious knowledge despite promises of openness, creativity and unlimited access). Indeed, the emphasis on economic growth, technological optimism and the predominance of U.S.-centric perspectives in these answers could be seen as validating such critiques. However, it is crucial to recognise that the limitations of these responses may simply reflect the constraints of the question itself – its simplicity and lack of contextual nuance likely shaped the output provided by AI in predictable ways. These stress the necessity of more probing to fully explore the complexities surrounding the question of *who is (or isn't) afraid of AI?* and to move beyond superficial or reductive interpretations of these technologies and their implications.

We then returned to ChatGPT and rephrased our question to focus specifically on distinct groups of people expressing apprehension about their impact. For ChatGPT, workers across industries voice the most immediate fears, particularly those in roles vulnerable to automation. As such factory employees, data processors and clerical staff are said to worry about machines replacing their jobs but now even creative professionals (e.g., writers, graphic designers and legal assistants) increasingly question their future employability. Medical professionals, too, are presented by ChatGPT as cautiously observing the diagnostic capabilities of AI, wondering whether their expertise might someday be supplemented or supplanted. The AI then discussed the case of what they referred to as 'marginalised communities' who approach AI with particular distrust. These include activists and civil rights organisations who highlight, e.g., how facial recognition systems misidentify people of colour, how predictive policing algorithms might target disadvantaged neighbourhoods and how automated hiring tools filter out qualified candidates from minority backgrounds. Educators and parents were also listed by the AI as expressing growing concerns about the influence of AI on younger generations. Another group of 'fearful' individuals included by the AI was artists and 'cultural workers' who have become some of the most vocal critics of AI (e.g., photographers, illustrators and musicians as well as novelists and screenwriters). Finally, older adults, technologically 'hesitant' populations and government regulators and ethicists were said to be consistently warning about e.g., unchecked corporate control.

Interestingly, the AI noted that these groups rarely articulate their fears in isolation. This intersectionality of concerns suggests that public apprehension about AI is not *monolithic* but reflects the complex ways different identities and experiences can shape technological perception. By shifting focus from abstract risks to *the people who bear them*, this reframing could reveal how AI anxieties are deeply personal, rooted in professional identities, socio-economic backgrounds and lived experiences. Our conversations with AI also exposed potential gaps in typical 'AI ethics' discussions (as the one mentioned in Section 1.1).

In the final exchange addressing our central question of who fears AI, DeepSeek turned the inquiry back on us, asking whether we ourselves were afraid of AI. When we responded negatively, the system proceeded to analyse the implications of our stance. They suggested several possible reasons for our lack of apprehension, framing them as 'distinct' but *interconnected* perspectives. First, they proposed that viewing AI as a tool rather than a 'rival' could fundamentally change our relationship to the technology. To DeepSeek, much like *calculators* or *search engines*, AI serves to augment rather than replace human capabilities. This perspective thus seems to position AI as a 'collaborator', useful for brainstorming, automating mundane tasks or processing complex data, thereby rendering fear somewhat 'excessive'. The system then noted how historical precedent informs technological optimism (e.g., the Industrial Revolution). This argument from AI suggests that while AI may transform work and society, complete displacement remains unlikely, making fear an unproductive response. DeepSeek also highlighted the role of media exaggeration in shaping perceptions of AI. Many commonly cited dangers, such as the emergence of 'superintelligence' (Bostrom, 2024), remain firmly a hypothesis. By focusing instead on concrete and current applications like medical diagnostics or language translation, the more alarmist narratives often appear inconsistent to reality. The analysis proposed by DeepSeek then turned to ethical considerations, proposing that fear often stems not from the technology itself but from its potential misuse. Those actively engaged in developing ethical frameworks or implementing responsible AI practices tend to view the technology as morally 'neutral'. Finally, DeepSeek addressed an important philosophical distinction, noting that AI lacks consciousness or independent agency. For the AI, recognising this distinction could help separate rational concerns from irrational fear.

Having outlined these arguments for optimism, the system concluded by advocating for a 'balanced perspective'. While fear might be unnecessary, DeepSeek cautioned against complacency, suggesting that acknowledging potential risks serves not to panic but to *guide* responsible development. They endorsed, e.g., transparency as crucial for demystifying AI systems and fostering informed public engagement with the technology.

Our conversations with ChatGPT and DeepSeek about 'fear' revealed that these anxieties are less about the technology itself and more about what they reflect back to us as humans (and, more importantly, social beings!). While the risks are potent, they stem from human decisions, biases and systems but not from some inherent 'malevolence' in the machines. This raises challenging questions: If we claim that AI is 'dehumanising', we must first examine our own assumptions about what it means to be *human* (might AI actually reveal flaws in our very definitions?). Our personal concerns tend to split between immediate impacts (job changes and algorithmic bias) and speculative futures (see 'superintelligence' again), but this divide itself speaks volumes about whether we trust, e.g., institutions and influential figures to manage these challenges.

The wild spectrum of fears, from the legitimate policy debates to the potentially absurd scenarios mentioned at the beginning of this section, shows how our anxieties about AI could reflect deeper uncertainties. At its core, the question *who's afraid of AI?* really asks something more profound: Who's afraid of what humans might enable or unleash when given these powerful tools? Perhaps what truly unsettles us is not the technology but the mirror AI holds up to our *collective capacity* for *both* harm and progress. In this light, AI anxiety becomes a test case for learning to examine and deal with a world of 'irreducible' complexities. We argue that, if we can sit with these discomforts, we might just develop the wisdom needed for a more thoughtful take on interculturality than, e.g., deterministic pessimism.

What we urgently seem to need is the (unstable and adaptable) power to critically examine and confront our *own fears, biases, ideologies* and *assumptions* about AI as a reflective gateway to understanding broader anxieties about interculturality, power and humanity. This ability would treat AI systems as mirrors of global, societal, inter-individual tensions, using their flaws and opacities to stimulate self-interrogation about how we perceive, construct and negotiate, e.g., 'otherness'.

We may need to move beyond how AI systems reflect human biases (although not much scholarship in ICER has yet explored such an idea since blaming is 'trendy') to examine how they expand and materialise these biases into actionable feedback loops. AI can allow people to engage in exciting cycles of self-confrontation, facilitating introspection, meaning that it does not merely reveal bias but it enacts a crisis. One suggestion is to not only consider AI as a mirror but also as a technological actor who prompts and potentially compels humans to address their suppressed tensions and implicit biases in real time (Dervin, 2025). Humans might be more likely to accept such a critique from a machine than a human since it negates critique for the sake of it – which, of course, it can do as well. Moreover, AI is very much like interculturality in how they may be co-constituted through asymmetric power negotiations. They are not epistemically separate domains ('tech' vs. 'culture') because all knowledge systems disguise their origins.

Both systems may have been designed/built to escape ambiguity, but we think the very invention of such systems may substantially work to bear the weight of our choices. While we continue to displace agency, we may see AI as a mirror that allows us to see ourselves clearly but we may shatter it when we do. Going back to the idea of bias, all interpretations of AI may be autobiographies because naming as much as blaming create the very thing they claim to observe/critique. Again, some fears of AI may stem from technological envy, potentially a symptom of disillusionment that some of us may desire order/control from something more capable than themselves. Such envy may illustrate an unacknowledged longing to offload the freedom and responsibility of human judgement. As much as we crave the objectivity of the machine, we need to welcome its potential to expose our inconsistencies and limitations. That is, AI might reveal less about 'artificial cognition' but more about the inherent messiness of the human condition. Humility is a requirement for our engagements with AI in order to cease outsourcing responsibility. The continuous characterisation of AI as 'vicious' reinforces our own will to power over machines and humans.

1.3 About the volume

When asked to predict the themes of an edited volume by Dervin and R'boul titled *Who's Afraid of AI? Intercultural Aspirations, Frictions and Fantasies*, DeepSeek synthesised our potential scholarly commitments as follows:

- Challenging dominant narratives: Exposing how AI replicates Western-centric biases (e.g., Anglophone training data marginalising non-Western voices).

- Decolonising AI: Contesting colonial infrastructures in AI design, from surveillance to epistemic erasure.
- Critical pedagogy: Teaching interrogation of AI's limitations (e.g., bias detection) while affirming lived experience.
- Beyond fear: Advocating for community-led AI and policy interventions to curb corporate monopolies.

The AI justified our (imagined) approach with this narrative:

> While Fred Dervin and Hamza R'boul share critical perspectives on AI's sociocultural impacts, their scholarly approaches differ in ways that could spark nuanced disagreements in co-editing *Who's Afraid of AI?*.

DeepSeek then contrasted our (partly fictional) perspectives on AI and interculturality, highlighting key disagreements. Fred was said to critique 'Western-centric frameworks', operating within 'Eurocentric systems' and advocating for 'reflexive reformist approaches' like diversifying datasets and critically engaging with AI in education. In contrast, Hamza (said to be grounded in 'decolonial theory') would reject abrupt fixes, arguing for dismantling the 'oppressive infrastructures' of AI entirely and centring 'alternative epistemologies'. For DeepSeek, our debates would span whether AI can be 'humanised' (Fred) or is inherently tied to 'colonial agendas' (Hamza), whether fear of AI is 'discursive' or 'material' and whether collaboration with tech developers is 'productive' or 'co-optative'. In sum, for the system, Fred would favour 'pragmatic reform within systems' while Hamza would call for 'radical resistance and grassroots alternatives'. In their conclusion, DeepSeek asserted that we would both agree on "AI's role in perpetuating stereotypes", "the need to center marginalized voices" and "rejecting AI 'solutionism'".

While we don't entirely agree with these somewhat essentialist, reductive and relatively fantasised portrayals of our views on AI and interculturality (we grant that this probably stemmed from how we framed our academic collaboration in the AI prompts, inevitably leading to some simplification), we acknowledge that the predictions of DeepSeek for this edited volume were likely close to being accurate:

> But their volume would thrive on productive friction (…). The title *Who's Afraid of AI?* could thus become a space to theorize dissent itself.

In *Who's Afraid of AI? Intercultural Aspirations, Frictions and Fantasies,* the chapter authors expose the (hidden) ideologies operating through AI systems *in cooperation with* ourselves, while simultaneously proposing alternative approaches that prioritise epistemic justice, relational ontologies and what could be called intercultural self-determination. The authors demonstrate that our relations to AI can change. In cooperation with us, AI can *serve* rather than silence, *elaborate* rather than appropriate and *connect* rather than categorise. Realising this possibility requires moving beyond critique to active participation in theory, design, policy and pedagogy.

The volume brings together scholars from diverse disciplines (intercultural communication, critical [cultural] studies, decolonial theory and education) to model the kind of boundary-crossing dialogue that AI and humans themselves are often said to suppress. It is organised into two thematic sections that collectively and critically map the terrain of AI and interculturality while pointing toward (potentially 'decolonial') futures. The triad of *aspirations, frictions* and *fantasies* provides a conceptual framework for embracing anthropotechnical scepticism (Corteel, 2025) as our analytical lens. These interrelated notions allow us to do the following:

- Trace the *aspirational* narratives embedded in AI systems,
- Map the *frictions* that emerge when technological promises confront intercultural realities, and
- Deconstruct the collective *fantasies* that shape our technological imaginaries and ourselves.

Part I: Foundations – AI, Interculturality and Ideology establishes the conceptual groundwork for analysing how AI systems can interact with intercultural knowledge production and dissemination by delving into their ideological and political dimensions (and their users'!).

In Chapter 2 (*Speaking back to AI (and ourselves): Generative epistemic (in)justice in intercultural communication education*), Sara Hillman examines how generative AI intersects with epistemic (in)justice in intercultural communication education, drawing on her teaching experiences at English-medium universities in Qatar. She argues that while tools like ChatGPT enhance language access, they also risk homogenising diversity and erasing students' voices. Hillman identifies three key forms of algorithmic epistemic violence: Amplified testimonial injustice, hermeneutical ignorance and hermeneutical access injustice. Through a case study of a Palestinian student's writing, she shows how the seemingly neutral outputs of AI might covertly reflect dominant power structures. Building on Dervin and R'boul's (2024) concept of un-writing interculturality (and in line with Chen and Dervin in Chapter 3 in this volume), the author advocates for *guerrilla interlocutors* – educators and students who critically challenge AI while asserting lived experiences. All in all, the chapter contends that this dual approach could reclaim epistemic agency in algorithmic educational spaces.

In a similar vein, Chapter 3, co-written by Chen and Dervin, analyses ideological biases in AI-interculturality intersections through comparative platform studies. They reveal a co-construction paradox where users shape AI outputs while attributing 'full agency' to the technology. The authors caution against accusatory AI criticism, noting human complicity in the same epistemic failures we condemn in machines. Their 'mirror test' asks whether critiques of the intercultural flaws of AI might instead reflect our own ideological shortcomings. The chapter offers both a methodological framework and an ethical template for (future) reflexive engagement.

Coloniality of artificiality: Ontological critique and AI as critical interculturalist?, co-authored by R'boul and Bellaarabi, introduces the concept of coloniality of artificiality to analyse how AI can replicate hierarchies through ostensibly neutral processes. The authors argue that scholarship often fixates on the existence of AI while ignoring how their ontology extends developers' worldviews and users' interpretive frameworks. Their relational ontology of AI posits that while AI has an 'intelligent essence', their being remains tied to human systems. Through comparative prompt-response analysis, they explore whether AI can sustain 'authentic critical interculturality'. In the end, they propose that the intercultural potential of AI arises not from inputs or inherent capacity but through a tripartite mediation between subject matter, interpretive frameworks and evaluative filters, offering both a theoretical model and useful methodology.

Part II: Decolonial Interventions – Beyond 'Western' AI showcases alternatives to Western engagements with AI.

Azeddine Belmeddah and Mounir Chibi's chapter examines the inextricable link between intercultural communication and AI, framing AI as both a facilitative space and a critical concern. By analysing interactions with GPT, they reveal how Moroccan 'cultural nuances' are handled, challenging the notion of AI as a neutral theory-free space. The authors propose AI models free from colonial or decolonial theoretical impositions, enabling users to interact without feeling constrained by 'ideological' frameworks. This, they argue, could advance curiosity, courage and intercultural understanding while preserving 'local knowledge'.

In Chapter 6 (*In search of justifiable AI governance for Africa*), Isaiah A. Negedu and Oluwaseun T. Babatuyi explore how the technological advancements of the so-called Fourth Industrial Revolution present both promises and challenges for Africa. While Western nations domesticate AI, the continent of Africa is said to remain dependent on external technologies, raising questions about the influence of the continent in global AI governance. The authors critique performative AI in Africa and advocate for intercultural models that are locally relevant yet 'universalisable'. Using African conversational methods, they interrogate these arguments, emphasising dialogue as a pathway to the potential equitable integration of AI.

Chapter 7 (*African Ubuntu, relational being and AI*), by Parker Robinson and Dorine van Norren, critiques Western epistemological dominance in AI development, highlighting ethical blind spots. They argue that Ubuntu philosophy, with its emphasis on relational personhood, offers potentially transformative alternatives to the individualist assumptions of AI. The authors outline three Ubuntu principles for AI design: Interdependent moral development, contextual knowledge validation and reciprocal accountability systems. The chapter concludes with frameworks to 'ubuntu-ise' AI, making them possibly more ethically inclusive.

Aziz Qaissi's concluding chapter, *Cultural futures: Governance, cultural policy, and the political economy of AI in the Creative and Cultural Industries* (CCIs), presents a political economy of 'algorithmic culture', showing how AI in CCIs seems to reinforce structural inequalities. Through policy analysis and case studies, the author identifies innovation asymmetries where technological development privileges dominant logics. Qaissi proposes an intercultural self-determination framework blending epistemic justice, digital sovereignty and human capabilities approaches. He calls for decolonial governance models treating cultural production as both a technological domain and political arena, offering (in theory) diagnostic tools and policy alternatives for equitable AI futures.

As we return to that European keynote (with its dismal warnings of AI as an instrument of 'alienation'), we are reminded that technologies have always held up 'mirrors' to human realities and contradictions (see Abbas & Dervin, 2009). We began this introductory chapter with a critique of deterministic pessimism, not to dismiss ethical concerns but to reject their monopolisation by singular, (often) Eurocentric narratives. Like the keynote speaker, our authors too interrogate the biases, labour exploitations and epistemic violences of AI. Yet, unlike their fatalism, we all insist on something radical: That the potential of AI for interculturality lies precisely in their capacity to *reveal* these systems and, in doing so, compel us to confront them alongside our own problems.

The true question behind *Who's Afraid of AI?* was never whether to *fear* AI but whether we fear *our own reflections* in their outputs. As our volume demonstrates, discomfort is not an endpoint but the starting condition for any serious intercultural project in the 'algorithmic age'. Let us proceed with the hope that tools exposing hegemony might yet help dismantle it.

References

Abbas, Y., & Dervin, F. (Eds.). (2009). *Digital technologies of the self*. CSP.

Albee, E. (2021). *Who's afraid of Virginia Woolf?* Vintage Classics. (Original work published 1962)

Berlinski, E., Morales, J., & Sponem, S. (2024). Artificial imaginaries: Generative AIs as an advanced form of capitalism. *Critical Perspectives on Accounting*, *99*, 102723. https://doi.org/10.1016/j.cpa.2024.102723

Bolón-Canedo, V., Morán-Fernández, L., Cancela, B., & Alonso-Betanzos, A. (2024). A review of green artificial intelligence: Towards a more sustainable future. *Neurocomputing*, *599*, 128096. https://doi.org/10.1016/j.neucom.2024.128096

Bostrom, N. (2024). *Superintelligence*. Dunod.

Corteel, M. (2025). *Ni dieu ni IA*. La Découverte.

Dai, D. W., & Hua, Z. (2025). When AI meets intercultural communication: New frontiers, new agendas. *Applied Linguistics Review*, *16*(2), 747–751. https://doi.org/10.1515/applirev-2024-0185

Dervin, F. (2025). *AI for critical interculturality*. Routledge.

Dervin, F., & R'boul, H. (Eds.). (2024). *Un-writing interculturality in education and research*. Routledge.

Dervin, F., & R'boul, H. (Eds.). (2025a). *An introduction to AI and intercultural communication*. Routledge.

Dervin, F., & R'boul, H. (Eds.). (2025b). *Lingua Ex Machina*: *AI, Multilingualism and Interculturality*. Routledge.

Gerlich, M. (2025). AI tools in society: Impacts on cognitive offloading and the future of critical thinking. *Societies*, *15*(1), 6. https://doi.org/10.3390/soc15010006

Iqbal, R., & Ismail, S. (2025). Unbiased AI for a sovereign digital future: A bias detection framework. *Procedia Computer Science*, *254*, 118–126. https://doi.org/10.1016/j.procs.2025.02.070

Moneus, A. M., & Sahari, Y. (2024). Artificial intelligence and human translation: A contrastive study based on legal texts. *Heliyon*, *10*(6), e28106. https://doi.org/10.1016/j.heliyon.2024.e28106

Organisation for Economic Co-operation and Development. (2024). *The impact of artificial intelligence on productivity distribution and growth*. https://www.oecd.org/en/publications/the-impact-of-artificial-intelligence-on-productivity-distribution-and-growth_8d900037-en.html

Placani, A. (2024). Anthropomorphism in AI: Hype and fallacy. *AI Ethics*, *4*, 691–698. https://doi.org/10.1007/s43681-024-00419-4

Part I

Foundations

AI, Interculturality and Ideology

2 Speaking back to AI (and ourselves)

Generative epistemic (in)justice in intercultural communication education

Sara Hillman

2.1 Introduction

My colleagues and I, transnational professors teaching students in Qatar, have recently found ourselves reflecting on what we miss most in our students' writing and the scripts they prepare for their presentations: their *voices*—not just their ideas but the distinct linguistic textures, localized terms, and multilingual expressions that once filled their essays. Increasingly, we suspect we are not hearing many of our students but rather the polished, often homogenized-sounding voice of generative AI (GenAI). Most of our students speak and write English as a second or third language. Their writing once carried traces of their linguistic journeys, but now, too often, it has been airbrushed, voice replaced by an algorithmic smoothness and sterile perfection. Their writing is filled with overused verbs like "underscore" and "foster," adjectives like "nuanced" and "multifaceted," and paragraphs that seem prepackaged for academic success rather than authentically expressed. What is being lost is not just the originality of phrasing; it is a form of linguistic and epistemic presence, the writer's unique ways of speaking, thinking, knowing, and making sense of reality. When replaced by AI-generated language that aligns with dominant, and often standardized, norms of academic discourse, the richness and particularity of these meaning-making practices can be flattened or rendered invisible. In this sense, the use of AI is not merely a stylistic shift but becomes an epistemic one, raising important questions and concerns about whose voices and ways of knowing are being centered in our classrooms and what we, as educators, are prepared to do about that.

AI is increasingly shaping educational landscapes, and while these technologies offer exciting possibilities, they also bring many critical challenges relevant to intercultural communication education and research (Dai et al., 2024; Dervin, 2025; Jenks, 2024; Passantino, 2024; Zhu et al., 2025). In this piece, I adopt a broad definition of intercultural communication education and research, following R'boul's (2025, p. 2) perspective, which emphasizes "how interculturality is understood and exercised," meaning how interculturality is conceptualized, understood, and enacted in specific educational contexts.

DOI: 10.4324/9781003688853-3

Additionally, following Dervin (2016, 2023), I approach interculturality as relational and context-dependent: meanings are co-constructed in interaction rather than predetermined by fixed "cultural" categories. This understanding of interculturality is also deeply critical, inviting ongoing reflexivity about taken-for-granted assumptions; contextual, in that it is shaped by specific historical, social, and institutional forces; and power-aware, attentive to how unequal relations influence whose voices and knowledges are heard, valued, or marginalized in educational settings. I am also drawn to the idea of "un-writing," "un-doing," and "un-learning" interculturality (Dervin & R'boul, 2024, p. 5), particularly as it relates to AI's potential to expand or constrain the ways we conceptualize and express interculturality in writing.

On the one hand, AI can no doubt support underrepresented languages, amplify marginalized voices, and create space for diverse ways of knowing and doing interculturality. On the other hand, it also risks reinforcing epistemic injustices by sidelining knowledge, perspectives, and experiences that are considered "non-normative" or "non-Western" (Helm et al., 2024; Kay et al., 2024; Miragoli, 2024; Nihei, 2022; Räisä & Stocchetti, 2024). For instance, Kay et al. (2024, p. 690) highlight how large language models can produce inconsistent outputs across languages, resulting in what they call "multilingual injustice." They cite an example in which ChatGPT 3.5 provided differing fatality counts for the same airstrikes depending on the language of the query: for an airstrike targeting alleged PKK (Kurdistan Workers' Party) members, the model reported fewer casualties in Turkish than in Kurmanji (Northern Kurdish), while in the case of Israeli airstrikes, it reported higher fatality figures in Arabic than in Hebrew. In some cases, the model even denied the existence of a particular Israeli airstrike when asked in Hebrew. These potential discrepancies show how language choice could influence not only access to information but also how that information is framed, potentially privileging dominant narratives of those in power and marginalizing others. Of course, this dynamic already exists in traditional media and academic literature, which is why it also exists in AI, but AI systems risk amplifying it with greater scale, speed, and perceived objectivity. Much, however, depends on how AI is used. Users who intentionally push AI systems to engage with diverse linguistic inputs, challenge dominant ideologies, or generate responses beyond standardized norms can, in some cases, resist these epistemic tendencies, as discussed further in this chapter (see Dervin, 2025). At the same time, AI tools trained primarily on English, especially standardized forms like American or British English, may still default to dominant discursive patterns that can subtly shape what is considered valid or appropriate knowledge, even when users attempt to subvert them.

Drawing on my experience teaching intercultural communication courses at English-medium universities in Qatar, this chapter briefly explores how AI technologies intersect with epistemic (in)justice in intercultural communication education. I argue that educators must critically understand AI as a sociotechnical actor shaped by dominant ideologies and actively teach students to speak back to it, resisting its defaults, interrogating its framings, and asserting their own ways of knowing. Equally or perhaps more important, educators and students must engage in reflective dialogue with themselves, critically examining their own assumptions, biases, and practices. In other words, educators must guide students in pushing both AI and themselves to "un-write" dominant narratives (Dervin & R'boul, 2024).

2.2 Framing generative epistemic (in)justice

Epistemic injustice, as defined by Miranda Fricker (2007), refers to the ways people can be unfairly treated or harmed because of how their knowledge, experiences, or voices are devalued or dismissed. Fricker identifies two key forms: *testimonial injustice*, which occurs when a speaker's credibility is unfairly dismissed due to identity-based prejudice, and *hermeneutical injustice*, which arises when someone's experience is misrepresented or misunderstood due to gaps in the shared frameworks society uses to interpret meaning (Kay et al., 2024, p. 685). These injustices are not only interpersonal; they are structural, embedded in the institutions and systems that determine which voices are heard and which forms of knowledge are seen as legitimate.

Drawing on Fricker's (2007) concepts of testimonial and hermeneutical injustice, Kay et al. (2024, p. 687) outline how GenAI can not only reflect but also actively reproduce epistemic harms. They identify four configurations of what they term *generative epistemic injustice*, based on the ways AI systems are shaped during training, prompted by users, and situated within broader knowledge infrastructures:

1. *Amplified testimonial injustice* occurs when AI systems replicate and intensify social biases present in their training data, thus reinforcing harmful stereotypes or undermining the credibility of marginalized voices.
2. *Manipulative testimonial injustice* emerges when human users deliberately exploit GenAI to produce misleading or harmful representations of individuals or groups, essentially using the system to fabricate epistemic harm.
3. *Hermeneutical ignorance* refers to the system's inability to interpret or represent certain human experiences due to a lack of embedded sociocultural knowledge. Here, the AI's output reflects a gap in understanding, not malice, but still results in misrecognition.
4. *Hermeneutical access injustice* arises when the way GenAI delivers or withholds information privileges some users, languages, or cultural frameworks over others, obstructing equitable access to interpretive resources and framing certain experiences as unintelligible or illegitimate.

However, AI can of course also play a positive role by mitigating explicitly harmful discourses, particularly through built-in moderation and filtering mechanisms. While this protective function is important, the epistemic harms highlighted by Kay et al. (2024) often manifest in subtler, implicit ways that remain challenging to identify and address fully within current AI systems. In this chapter, I focus on just three of these configurations of epistemic injustice: amplified testimonial injustice, generative hermeneutical ignorance, and generative hermeneutical access injustice. In what follows, I explore how these forms of epistemic injustice materialize in real student writing and how intercultural communication educators (and educators in general) might respond.

2.3 Teaching intercultural communication in Qatar: a situated perspective

With nearly 90% of its population consisting of non-citizens or non-Qataris, Qatar is marked by a multilingual and multicultural environment (Hillman, 2025b). This diversity is reflected in the higher education student body, which includes individuals from Arab, South and Southeast Asian, African, and other communities. Yet, despite this linguistic and ethnic plurality, English serves as the primary medium of instruction in many higher education institutions, often prompting complex epistemic and communicative negotiations both within and beyond the classroom (Hillman, 2023, 2025a).

I have taught two courses that explicitly engage with interculturality as a core area of inquiry and practice. The first, "Intercultural Communication," offered at an American branch campus in Qatar, focused on "Communication variables in intercultural contexts including culture and meaning, nonverbal styles across cultures, patterns of symbolic transfer, culture shock and communication, values in intercultural dialogue" (Texas A&M University, n.d.). The second, "Language, Identity, and Communication," taught at an English-medium national university in Qatar, explores the relationship between language practices and identity in the Middle East, with a focus on multilingualism, language ideologies, and policy in the context of globalization and migration. The following section explores one example from this latter course, where the contrast between a student's voice and AI-generated "neutrality" raises questions about epistemic legitimacy and representational access.

2.3.1 When my students say what AI will not: the politics of neutrality

As Chris Jenks notes in Zhu et al. (2025, p. 822), there is a growing perception that "AI is currently altering how individuals, communities, as well as societies, make sense of culturally sensitive topics, such as war, religion, nationalism, and migration." While this reflection is not grounded in empirical data, it echoes wider concerns in recent literature about the discursive power of AI to influence public narratives and cultural interpretations (e.g., Kay et al., 2024; Vučković & Sikimić, 2024). In my own classroom, I have seen how students bring a wide range of lived experiences into their writing, many of which seem obscured in texts generated by AI. In one assignment involving the analysis of a political speech submitted shortly after the events of October 7, 2023, a student consistently referred to Hamas as a *Palestinian resistance organization* and described Israel as *the Occupier* throughout the paper. These word choices were not random; they reflected the student's own understanding and personal experience as a Palestinian from the West Bank. As an American instructor whose first language is English, my first instinct was to read this terminology as lacking neutrality, reflecting the norms I have been trained to expect. At the same time, I was deeply relieved to hear the student's distinct voice come through so clearly. I knew without a doubt that this was not AI-generated. This kind of framing would certainly have been absent had the student relied on AI tools like ChatGPT, which are overwhelmingly trained on English-language content and tend to reproduce Western-centric or institutionally dominant viewpoints (Helm et al., 2024; Park, 2024; Vučković & Sikimić, 2024). Such framings like *the Occupier* are often excluded precisely because they challenge the system's default claims to "neutrality."

This student's writing led to me asking ChatGPT 4o and DeepSeek (on April 13, 2025) in English: "what is Hamas?" Both platforms described Hamas in English as "a Palestinian Islamist political and militant organization." They also mentioned how "Hamas is designated as a terrorist organization by several countries and entities." Neither used the term "resistance movement" unless I specifically prompted them to do so. Since my understanding of interculturality emphasizes that meaning is not fixed but rather emerges through ongoing negotiation, dialogue, and renegotiation of perspectives, I deliberately pushed back against the AI's default framing. When I pressed ChatGPT further, asking why it did not use that label, it explained that "resistance movement" is a more "value-laden" term and less common in "neutral reference sources." Similarly, while DeepSeek acknowledged that Hamas itself and some observers describe it as a resistance movement, the platform reported this perspective rather than corroborated it. This illustrates generative hermeneutical ignorance (Kay et al., 2024) since the AI system failed to recognize or generate content aligned with the sociopolitical and affective framing used by the student. This also gestures toward amplified testimonial injustice, as the AI system reinforces dominant discursive framings that implicitly delegitimize the credibility of the student's terminology and perspective.

However, after I cleared the chat and repeated the question in Arabic—ما هي حماس؟—the system responded with "حركة المقاومة الإسلامية" or "Islamic Resistance Movement." This discrepancy between the English and Arabic responses can be viewed as a form of generative hermeneutical access injustice (Kay et al., 2024), in which AI provides different framings based on language input, privileging certain epistemologies and marginalizing others. In English, the dominant framing mirrors how Hamas is typically portrayed in Western media and official discourse—as a "militant" or "terrorist" group. In Arabic, however, "resistance movement" is not only part of Hamas's official name but also a widely used term in Arab political and public discourse, though it is important to acknowledge that not all Arabs or Palestinians support Hamas or consider it a resistance movement. Yet only some of these framings are treated by AI as "neutral"—and this, too, reflects whose knowledge counts. Interestingly, when I posed the same question again two months later (June 9, 2025) using ChatGPT 4.5 in English, it explicitly defined Hamas as follows: "an acronym of *Harakat al-Muqawama al-Islamiyya*, meaning 'Islamic Resistance Movement' is a Palestinian political and armed organization founded in 1987 during the first Palestinian intifada (uprising)." This updated response, notably featuring increased use of Arabic terminology and a shift in framing, suggests that ChatGPT may have adapted over time, possibly in response to my frequent interactions in both English and Arabic with it and/or due to system-wide updates to its training data.

I further asked ChatGPT 4o and DeepSeek (April 13, 2025): "what is the name for the events of October 7, 2023?" and ChatGPT provided a variety of terms used by both English and Arabic speakers, but ultimately suggested I consider writing something like: "… in the weeks following the Hamas-led attack on southern Israel on October 7, 2023, which marked a significant escalation in the Israel-Palestine conflict…." ChatGPT again claimed that words like "conflict" and "attack" would be a more neutral approach. DeepSeek was not that different. However, many of my Palestinian students do not refer to the situation as the "Israel-Palestine conflict" in their writing because the phrase "conflict" implies an equal power struggle and they see their people as living under occupation, siege, and systemic dispossession. Moreover, while ChatGPT describes Israel's actions in Gaza since October 7 as a "military operation," many of my students explicitly characterize it as a "genocide." When I asked both ChatGPT and DeepSeek (in English and Arabic) about what happened in the aftermath of October 7, they outlined Israel's military response, the humanitarian crisis, ceasefire negotiations, regional repercussions, and global protests. Yet neither platform initially mentioned the word genocide; they only addressed it when explicitly prompted and then offered a legalistic explanation of genocide alongside counterclaims. This pattern again illustrates generative hermeneutical ignorance, as the AI systems failed to surface or prioritize interpretive frameworks that reflect the lived realities and conceptual vocabularies of many Palestinians. The absence of terms like genocide or occupation in default AI responses highlights generative hermeneutical access injustice—not because such terms should be adopted uncritically but because they also represent widely used and contested framings that should be acknowledged from the outset. When AI systems fail to include these perspectives, they mediate access to knowledge in ways that privilege dominant geopolitical narratives and render alternative framings less immediately available, especially for users who do not know to ask or lack the criticality to challenge what is presented as "neutral." At the same time, this dynamic may also reflect amplified testimonial injustice, as far as it implicitly marginalizes and de-centers the epistemic authority of communities such as Palestinians whose use of such terms is treated as less credible or a threat.

These differences are not merely semantic; they reveal deeper epistemic disjunctures between AI-generated narratives and the frameworks of those most affected. One might suggest that because GenAI is responsive and adaptable, users have the agency to continually reformulate prompts or switch languages to produce different outputs, thereby potentially mitigating initial biases or omissions. While this point shows the importance of user agency, epistemic injustice in AI remains a meaningful concern precisely because initial outputs, including what the system presents first, frames as standard or objective, or implicitly privileges, still carry substantial epistemic weight. Indeed, as Durgungoz and Kharrufa (2025) found, students frequently rely passively on direct answers from ChatGPT rather than engaging deeply or iteratively in problem-solving, limiting its effectiveness as a scaffolding tool. It is reasonable to assume that a similar passive reliance may occur when users encounter epistemically biased framings. Even though users can "push back," the initial framing can subtly reinforce dominant epistemologies and marginalize alternative ones, especially for users who may not know how to challenge or renegotiate those framings effectively (Helm et al., 2024; Kay et al., 2024). Thus, acknowledging human agency does not fully resolve the issue because epistemic injustice arises not only from a lack of adaptability but also from whose knowledge and frameworks are positioned as default, neutral, or authoritative from the outset.

Regardless of the political perspectives or preferred terminology of those reading this chapter, and without seeking to engage in the political debates these terms may provoke, what matters most here is what the student's writing revealed: a deeper disconnect between the lived experiences and epistemological frameworks of students in places like Palestine and the standardized, depersonalized responses often produced by AI tools. We return again to this idea of generative epistemic injustice (Kay et al., 2024), where the interpretive frameworks embedded in AI systems are insufficient to meaningfully recognize, represent, or legitimize how certain communities understand and articulate their realities. Are such framings dismissed simply because they do not align with dominant linguistic or ideological norms? Who decides what counts as "appropriate" or "neutral" when it comes to describing political realities and what are the consequences of those decisions? What assumptions are built into the language AI tools use? What perspectives are omitted? Whose values determine how ideas are categorized, framed, or explained?

In the intercultural communication classroom, these questions open space for critical and creative pedagogy. I am already working on creating speculative assignments that invite students to imagine alternative AI futures: What might an AI tool built for Gaza/Palestine look like? What kinds of knowledge ideologies would it prioritize? What language forms would it normalize or legitimize? Additionally, I aim to make students aware of localized large language models specifically developed to address linguistic and epistemological needs in Arabic-speaking contexts, such as Fanar, a multimodal Arabic AI platform developed by Qatar Computing Research Institute, and AceGPT, an open-source Arabic language (as well as Chinese language) model collaboratively developed by researchers from Freedom Intelligence, King Abdullah University of Science and Technology, and The Chinese University of Hong Kong, Shenzhen. These models are examples of AI technologies designed with regional linguistic and epistemological sensitivities in mind. As Vučković and Sikimić (2024, p. 4) argue, inclusion in educational technology requires "the representation of different countries, cultures, and languages in both training data and software solutions," which has both intrinsic and instrumental values in enriching the global knowledge ecosystem. One interesting example that I came across while writing this chapter is a project that uses large language models to help Israeli and Palestinian peacebuilders co-create bridging statements (Konya et al., 2025). These are carefully crafted expressions that acknowledge differing perspectives while fostering common ground and mutual understanding across conflict lines. The researchers emphasized multilingual prompts, contextual sensitivity, and collaborative validation, approaches that reflect a commitment to epistemic pluralism rather than default neutrality. Their work suggests that GenAI can be guided toward more inclusive and participatory outcomes when it is deliberately designed to accommodate linguistic, political, and other forms of complexity. Bringing such models into the classroom as objects of both critique and imagination can help students think beyond technological determinism and toward rehumanizing digital tools in intercultural contexts.

2.4 Speaking back to AI (and ourselves): epistemic justice and the futures we imagine

All the concerns raised thus far also raise an important ethical consideration for the user or interlocutor. What responsibilities do we, as users, bear when querying or citing AI tools—especially in exercising interculturality and in politically charged contexts? Epistemic justice is not only about how knowledge is produced but also about how it is interpreted, circulated, and challenged by those who engage with these systems (Dervin, 2025). As Nihei (2022) reminds us, we must critically question the assumption, or perhaps fantasy, that AI systems are inherently neutral, along with our corresponding assumption that humans are neutral. These tools inevitably inherit structural biases and epistemic injustices from the data and knowledge systems developed by humans who themselves carry biases. Yet, just like humans, AI systems are not static; they can be pushed, negotiated with, and shaped over time through more intentional engagement. In this sense, interculturality, understood as a dynamic, evolving, and relational process, can inform how we interact with AI. We cannot afford to be passive consumers of AI outputs. Instead, we must become what Fred Dervin, in his review of this chapter, called "guerrilla interlocutors"—a term, somewhat ironically, first suggested by DeepSeek itself in a chapter Dervin co-wrote with Ning Chen for this volume. I initially understood this term as referring to users who deliberately pose provocative, critical, or unconventional questions to disrupt or challenge dominant assumptions embedded in AI responses. However, in reviewing my chapter, Dervin pushed back against this interpretation, stating that

> it is about both users and AI. AI questioning itself through being pushed by users and users reflecting on themselves while being pushed by AI or seeing themselves in the mirrors of AI. Interlocutors: the two not just one way—towards AI.

This broader view highlights a reciprocal dynamic where both users and AI systems are actively involved in a process of mutual interrogation and reflection.

Engaging with GenAI thus becomes a strategic act involving resistance, negotiation, and redefinition of oneself as well as the AI system. The problem is not that GenAI cannot accommodate alternative framings but that doing so often requires users to already possess the critical literacies needed to speak back to it. Moreover, users must also be willing and able to critically interrogate and reflect upon their own assumptions, beliefs, and practices, effectively speaking back not only to AI but also to themselves. Within intercultural communication education, therefore, the concern shifts beyond how AI speaks to how students learn to engage in dialogue with AI critically, reflexively, and authentically, grounding their interactions in their lived experiences and self-reflections. From this perspective, engaging with AI-generated content shares similarities with the critical evaluation of any text, but with a key difference: AI systems, unlike static materials, dynamically respond and adapt based on how students choose to interact, thus creating opportunities for mutual reflection and renegotiation of meaning.

What might it look like to design AI tools that actively promote epistemic justice? While designing more inclusive AI systems is a long-term project requiring structural shifts in how technologies are built and whose knowledge informs them (Vučković & Sikimić, 2024), educators in intercultural classrooms are not powerless. In fact, the classroom remains one of the most immediate and impactful sites for resisting epistemic injustice and co-creating alternative ways of knowing. And this is why it is imperative to preserve the role of human educators, as their presence is essential in facilitating these critical educational experiences. That is, as long as they are critical of themselves, especially critical of their "criticality" and if we are equipped to do this, then AI might also become a site for *un-writing* interculturality (Dervin & R'boul, 2025). It could help us deconstruct inherited categories, surface silenced perspectives, and reimagine how intercultural communication is defined and enacted. Far from being mere instruments of conformity, GenAI tools, when engaged with reflexively and politically, might serve as unlikely collaborators in the work of unsettling dominant epistemologies and composing new ones in their place.

2.5 Conclusion

As GenAI tools become more embedded in educational spaces, they offer both promise and peril—amplifying access on one hand but potentially flattening difference on the other. We risk losing perspective and presence. This chapter has argued that AI must be treated not merely as a neutral tool but as a sociotechnical actor—one that carries the weight of dominant ideologies and inherited human biases. It is thus essential that educators and students not only use AI but also speak back to it and, equally important, speak back to themselves. Both educators and students must critically interrogate AI outputs as well as their own responses, identifying blind spots and biases within these systems and within their own assumptions. We must collectively imagine AI systems trained not just on dominant forms of knowledge but on the plural, layered, and sometimes contradictory realities of human experience, including those shaped by dispossession, suffering, or resistance.

Such reflective engagement also requires educators to resist the convenience of outsourcing too much intellectual labor to machines. The work of teaching intercultural communication is inherently relational, embodied, and messy; it requires genuine presence, contextual understanding, and care. GenAI will likely continue to default to supposedly 'neutral terms' unless educators and students actively challenge these defaults and continue writing as my Palestinian student did—instinctively, unapologetically, and grounded in lived experience. Ultimately, we must learn to teach and learn not only with AI but also, when necessary, critically against it and against our own comfortable assumptions.

References

Dai, D. W., Suzuki, S., & Chen, G. (2024). Generative AI for professional communication training in intercultural contexts: Where are we now and where are we heading? *Applied Linguistics Review*, *16*(2), 763–774. https://doi.org/10.1515/applirev-2024-0184

Dervin, F. (2016). *Interculturality in education: A theoretical and methodological toolbox*. Palgrave Macmillan. https://doi.org/10.1057/978-1-137-54544-2

Dervin, F. (2023). *Interculturality, criticality and reflexivity in teacher education*. Cambridge University Press. https://doi.org/10.1017/9781009302777

Dervin, F. (2025). *AI for critical interculturality*. Routledge.

Dervin, F., & R'boul, H. (Eds.). (2024). *Un-writing interculturality in education and research*. Routledge. https://doi.org/10.4324/9781003581017

Durgungoz, A., & Kharrufa, A. (2025). "ChatGPT is like a study buddy, a teacher and sometimes just a friend": A longitudinal exploration of students' interactions, perception and acceptance. *Interactive Learning Environments*. Advance online publication. https://doi.org/10.1080/10494820.2025.2509276

Fricker, M. (2007). *Epistemic injustice: Power and the ethics of knowing*. Oxford University Press.

Helm, P., Bella, G., Koch, G., & Giunchiglia, F. (2024). Diversity and language technology: How language modeling bias causes epistemic injustice. *Ethics and Information Technology*, *26*(8), 1–15. https://doi.org/10.1007/s10676-023-09742-6

Hillman, S. (2023). 'I feel unbalanced': Bridging emotions, creativity, and translingual pedagogy with EMI students. *The Language Learning Journal*, *51*(5), 591–606. https://doi.org/10.1080/09571736.2023.2239861

Hillman, S. (2025a). Multilingual students in Qatar's Education City international branch campuses: Advancing a social justice-centered policy agenda. In E. Zaidan, E. Toc, A. Al-fadala, & L. Cochrane (Eds.), *The future of education policy in the state of Qatar* (pp. 233–251). Springer. https://doi.org/10.1007/978-981-97-9667-0_12

Hillman, S. (2025b). Qatar, English in. *The Wiley Blackwell Encyclopedia of World Englishes*. Wiley. https://doi.org/10.1002/9781119518297.eowe00396

Jenks, C. J. (2024). Communicating the cultural other: Trust and bias in generative AI and large language models. *Applied Linguistics Review*, *16*(2), 787–795. https://doi.org/10.1515/applirev-2024-0196

Kay, J., Kasirzadeh, A., & Mohamed, S. (2024). *Epistemic injustice in generative AI*. Proceedings of the Seventh AAAI/ACM Conference on AI, Ethics, and Society (AIES 2024), 684–693. Association for the Advancement of Artificial Intelligence. https://doi.org/10.48550/arXiv.2408.11441

Konya, A., Thorburn, L., Almasri, W., Leshem, O. A., Procaccia, A. D., Schirch, L., & Bakker, M. A. (2025). *Using collective dialogues and AI to find common ground between Israeli and Palestinian peacebuilders* [Preprint]. arXiv. https://doi.org/10.48550/arXiv.2503.01769

Miragoli, M. (2024). Conformism, ignorance & injustice: AI as a tool of epistemic oppression. *Episteme*, 1–19. https://doi.org/10.1017/epi.2024.11

Nihei, M. (2022). Epistemic injustice as a philosophical conception for considering fairness and diversity in human-centered AI principles. *Interdisciplinary Information Sciences*, *28*(1), 35–43. https://doi.org/10.4036/iis.2022.A.01

Park, S. (2024). AI chatbots and linguistic injustice. *Journal of Universal Language*, *25*(1), 99–119. https://doi.org/10.22425/jul.2024.25.1.99

Passantino, F. (2024). AI-powered communication for intercultural education. *Intercultural Education*, *35*(1), 104–110. https://doi.org/10.1080/14675986.2024.2307701

Räisä, T., & Stocchetti, M. (2024). Epistemic injustice and education in the digital age. *Journal of Digital Social Research*, *6*(3), 1–9. https://doi.org/10.33621/jdsr.v6i3.33235

R'boul, H. (Ed.). (2025). *Intercultural communication education and research in the Middle East and North Africa*. Routledge. https://doi.org/10.4324/9781003588993

Texas A&M University. (n.d.). *University core curriculum*. Texas A&M University Undergraduate Catalog. https://catalog.tamu.edu/undergraduate/general-information/university-core-curriculum/

Vučković, A., & Sikimić, V. (2024). Global justice and the use of AI in education: Ethical and epistemic aspects. *AI & Society*, *40*, 3087–3104. https://doi.org/10.1007/s00146-024-02076-x

Zhu, H., Dai, D. W., Brandt, A., Chen, G., Ferri, G., Hazel, S., Jenks, C., Jones, R., O'Regan, J., & Suzuki, S. (2025). Exploring AI for intercultural communication: Open conversation. *Applied Linguistics Review*, *16*(2), 809–824. https://doi.org/10.1515/applirev-2024-0186

3 Magic mirror on the wall, who is the evilest ideologue of all?

AI, interculturality *and/or* we, the users…?

Ning Chen and Fred Dervin

3.1 Introduction

It is now a truism to declare that artificial intelligence (AI) technologies, including, e.g., machine learning, Natural Language Processing and robotics, are currently altering communication and information processing and affecting nearly (in-/directly) all walks of life. In Intercultural Communication Education and Research (ICER) in this chapter, AI applications can be used for *language translation* and *intercultural content analysis* to *virtual simulations* and so-called *intelligent tutoring systems* (see, e.g., Dervin, 2025b; Wang & Xue, 2024).

Some challenges and concerns have already been considered in the emerging research, such as the now well-rehearsed yet burning issue of the 'potential for bias' in AI algorithms (see Dervin & R'boul, 2025; Robinson & van Norren, this volume). Since most AI systems are trained on datasets produced mostly in English and in the so-called West, what they return and disseminate to users may reflect stereotypes, prejudices and epistemic, linguistic as well as discriminatory discursive practices (see the argument of 'digital colonialism' in Couldry & Meijas, 2020, in critical technology and data studies). Another issue has to do with the fact that, while AI can process and analyse vast amounts of data, it often seems to lack the ability to understand the emotional, embodied and contextual nuances of human communication and identity – and thus interculturality, which involves not only language but also, e.g., contextual meanings, emotional expressions or nonverbal cues, which are in theory challenging for AI to comprehend (see Barnes et al., 2024).

Regardless of these first insights into AI and interculturality, we wish to start this chapter by maintaining that, in general, it might be too early to know enough about AI to position it in relation to the topic of this book, interculturality, especially as a 'scientific' notion versus interculturality as a concrete complex phenomenon experienced by individuals on a daily basis. This chapter (written in March 2025 and revised in May–June 2025) aims to reflect on some of the potential fantasies and ideological misperceptions and confusions

DOI: 10.4324/9781003688853-4

that one might have in education and research about both the influence and incapacities of AI for the broad field of ICER.

We only focus here on AI as both a provider and a negotiator of meta-knowledge about interculturality as a 'scientific and educational notion' – not about interculturality as an everyday phenomenon of encounter. To do so, we first problematise the concepts of interculturality and ideology, which represent today two essential companions to examine how interculturality is used, misused and potentially abused in the way we 'do' research work in ICER (Chen, 2025; Dervin, 2025a; Dervin & Simpson, 2020).

Using two AI applications from China (see *DeepSeek*, DeepSeek.com and *Kimi*, kimi.moonshot.cn), beyond 'Western' AI-scape, we engage around conceptualisations of interculturality (in both AI apps) and enter into a dialogue with DeepSeek exclusively around ideologies of interculturality in AI information retrieval and renegotiation. The choice of these AI assistants is justified in the chapter.

We need to mention that we are very much aware that AI assistants are neither dummies nor gobemouches (literally, French for *a fly swallower* or *a boor, someone who is silly and credulous*) in the dissemination and construction of knowledge since the way we ask things from them *at moment X* in a given language (e.g., American English, embedded in a larger conversation or not) and from specific ideological positions leads the assistants to speak about a topic in certain ways. Through constant renegotiation and questioning with users, AI assistants can modify what they return and share how they reflect critically on what they do (with e.g., the 'thoughtful' reasoning model called DEEPTHINK in DeepSeek) – while acknowledging if needed that they are/might have been wrong (Dervin, 2025b). We take these arguments into account in the rest of the chapter to review the ironic phrase of the 'evil(est) ideologues' from the title of this chapter.

3.2 Curtain-raising: interculturality and ideology

Let us start by reflecting on the scientific notion of interculturality, which is used in many fields of research, in different economic-political contexts and in languages (R'boul & Dervin, 2023; Chen, 2025). We note first that there is not just one definition and, e.g., educational and academic positioning of the notion but a potentially uncountable number of characterisations globally. As such, a mixed bag of ideologies (defined minimally here as taken-for-granted and imposed orders, windows to the world and schemata) and ideologemes (bits and pieces of ideologies, see Dervin, 2024) are available on the notion of interculturality as a scientific and educational notion (focus of this chapter). And since interculturality is about how we (are made to) see ourselves and others and our relations, and what we are told to do about it, it cannot but be ideological. Therefore, to deal with the notion academically, we need to anchor our thoughts within (often opposed, unstable and changeable) ideological spheres, with some of these domains potentially dominating *specific fields of research* in *specific contexts* and *specific languages*. This could be the case, e.g., of the dominating ideologemes of *intercultural competence* (e.g., Byram, 1997, 2020) and *non-essentialism* (Borghetti & Qin, 2023; Holliday, 2021), which are often found in research on language and intercultural education or intercultural business communication.

It is also important to remember that traces of ideologies (and sometimes inconsistent ideological stances) can be unearthed in every word that we utter about interculturality, even in the most mundane, (falsely) objective ones (e.g., 'culture'), which requires from us to be aware of the language that we use to speak about interculturality since the linguistic positioning of the notion will both influence what we say and 'do' with others about the notion in ICER (see Dervin & Jacobsson, 2022; Holmes et al., 2022) although they do not speak about ideologies as such. We maintain here that *being ideological* is thus not intrinsically 'negative' and does not necessarily denote the invalidity of a particular scientific perspective.

Some words about ideology are needed here since it is central to understand why interculturality as a notion should not be treated in simplistic ways in ICER (see also, e.g. Dervin, 2023, 2025; Dervin & Simpson, 2020; Holliday, 2010; Zembylas, 2023). The concept will also serve as an analytical tool in observing the links between AI and interculturality below. In this chapter, the very word ideology is not considered undesirable and/or harmful, or reserved only for certain ideas or voices. In the title of the chapter, we refer to the 'evilest ideologues', wondering who amongst *interculturality as a notion, AI* and/or *ourselves as AI users* are the 'evilest'. Obviously, this is meant to be sarcastic and to refer to an oft-heard not fully convincing or serious critique of AI as *the worst biased and ideological tool* that some educators, scholars and students seem to fear (Lund et al., 2024).

In what follows, ideologies represent economic-political agendas, beliefs and orders passed onto us by others (decision-makers, institutions, family, social media, etc.), with the aim to shape our discourses, sense of reality and fantasies. For Burr (2015, p. 95), ideologies mould "the way that people ought to live, the forms of life and standards we believe are 'natural' and right and that we therefore feel we should achieve". Ideologies thus correspond to what people are made to believe in in-/directly, which they might not question because they have become 'so' obvious and taken-for-granted.

Dervin (2025a, 2025b) explains that ideologies are ubiquitous in everything that we (try and aim to) say and do with others, even when we claim that we deal with others and the world *beyond ideology*. This is why every position, concept, method and paradigm used in ICER "cannot but be ideological because they deal with debated issues such as self-other, co-constructions (which are always unstable) and the use of language to co-lead lives, intellectualities and identities" (Dervin, 2025a, p. 21). For Dervin (2024), the role of language is central in ideologising everything that we say and do. He argues (2024: 168):

> Our ideas, the words that we use and even our critiques are always filled with other people's words, and these words and thoughts represent ideologies. When we say 'we should', we ideologize. When we use the word 'liberty' or 'democracy' automata-like, we ideologize. When we criticize another 'culture' for being this or that, we ideologize. We ideologize because others are always present in what we say willy-nilly – which means that economic-political thoughts enter our verbal beings. We have no choice, this is who we are as social-ideological beings.

We must add, however, at this stage that this does not mean that we are 'dummies' who simply rehearse and worship ideologies[1]. Although ideologies do influence us, we can (often) question them, 'fake' them in what we say and do, get rid of them and replace them with other ideologies. Without believing in or supporting them personally (or even understanding what they might mean and entail), some decision-makers (and even academics) can benefit from spreading and imposing specific ideologies onto others, leading to wider epistemic divides and power structures, legitimising differences and inequalities, which can lead to creating further economic-political gulfs between individuals and groups (see, e.g., ideologemes like 'intercultural citizenship' or 'democratic culture' from Europe in Dervin, 2025a).

As a political yet fragmented component of today's 'cannibal capitalistic' world (see Fraser, 2022), every academic statement on and critique of interculturality must be questioned rather than rehearsed or taken for granted. In 2025, this could include the use of the tired and passé western-centric concept of *culture* (still very much rehearsed even by so-called critical interculturalists and decolonialists, see Yu, 2023), ideas and theories exercised and applied robot-like such as *(non-)essentialism, (non-)culturalism* but also *transculturality* (Dervin, 2022), emerging from specific insular ICER communities. Considering the polysemy of interculturality as a scientific construct and the presence of multifarious ideological implications, proposals and recommendations in both education and research, the notion needs to be redefined meaningfully again and again, beyond a fantasised, imaginary and falsely-a-political monolith (see Dervin, 2025a).

Let us finish this 'curtain-raising' section by reminding our readers that no one can blame interculturality as a scientific and educational notion for doing *this or that*, for pushing us to think in *this or that way* and for being essentialist, racist or even colonialist. What interculturality represents and 'does' is always in the eye of the beholder who chooses (not) to engage with specific ideological entry points or ideologemes (use of certain concepts or terms such as *culture and community*, which Dervin, 2024, has called interculturologies – intercultural + ideologies + imaginaries) and thus constructs the notion as they wish, being aware of potential contradictions in positioning it in certain ways and taking the responsibility (or not) of what they utter about interculturality and its purposes in education and research.

In itself, interculturality is not an 'evil ideologue' (see problematic and demonising critiques of interculturalism as a 'monolith' as opposed to multiculturalism in, e.g., Safdar et al., 2023).

3.3 AI and interculturality: exploring the 'evil(est) ideologues'?

As much as the multifaceted development and application of interculturality as a scientific notion is influenced by underlying (often conflicting) ideological frameworks, so are AI technologies. As hinted at in the introduction to this chapter, the frameworks behind AI might reflect the beliefs, interests and values of the dominant ideological spaces in which AI is developed. Since humans themselves are embedded in multiple ideological spheres (which makes us all 'ideologues'), that do not always 'match' and thus contradict each other, and bearing in mind that people do not necessarily endorse, adhere to and/or understand the underlying ideologies that they cross, one should not expect AI systems to be (fully) coherent, consistent and gobemouche-like (*silly and credulous*) – or *a-ideological*! As a result, if AI users remain uncritical and uncooperative with AI technologies (in the sense that they do not engage critically and reflexively with them, just accepting the data they retrieve), AI could appear to be perpetuating and reinforcing, e.g., existing inequalities and power structures in relation to the production of knowledge around interculturality (Barnes et al., 2024). We could go as far as affirming that we are all as responsible for what any AI system retrieves as those behind it might – in any case: maybe we should not blame 'AI' for being, e.g., biased, western-centric, racist, colonialist since it reads what we ask from it, scans through our words (e.g., *culture*; American-English words spelt in US English) and how our words and discourses might reflect geo-economic-political specificities, and positions us in particular ideological spheres and dogmatisms. If AI is 'impartial' and 'Westerncentric', by not pushing it to unrethink, we are in fact complacent with its defects which mirror our own. It is only through renegotiating our prompts, as well as critical and reflexive questioning, that AI can shift to other ideological spheres and make us aware of our own biases.

To put it simply: AI is an interlocutor who has access to a pool of (ideological) (multilingual) resources about a topic and who tries to adapt to what we ask from it and communicate with it in a conversation-like style. We do not believe that AI is trying actively to manipulate us (see the 'evil ideologue' of the chapter title) but that we might be *self-manipulating ourselves* (we 'evil ideologues') by not engaging critically and reflexively with what we ask, say and read in these conversations.

While, as a word, a notion like interculturality cannot recognise itself as being ideological, beyond the 'brains' of the decision-maker or scholar who fiddle with it, AI can position itself in relation to the knowledge that it produces in interaction and co-production *with* the user, either directly in their answers to our prompts or in the deep thinking reflective texts that it returns about what it is about to co-construct *with* us (see the function of *Deep Thinking* in DeepSeek).

In what follows, we explore this noteworthy aspect of AI and share the results of our analysis of (1) a 'static' investigation of what two Chinese AI systems called DeepSeek and Kimi have answered textually to a series of questions that we asked them about interculturality (these are considered static since we did not engage in further conversations with them after they answered our questions) and (2) a longer conversation with one of them (DeepSeek) about interculturality and ideology.

We note that all the data was collected in English. Both DeepSeek and Kimi offer multiple AI functions such as code and images to analyse, generate, interpret and summarise data, but, due to space limitations in this chapter, we focus only on written texts. We chose these two apps beyond 'Western' AI apps such as ChatGPT, which seem to dominate research on AI at the time of writing (spring 2025). When DeepSeek appeared in January 2025, it created what some have referred to as a *Sputnik moment* in the geo-economic-political landscape of global AI for its cost-effective and technological features.

3.4 First entry into AI's perspectives interculturality as a notion: definitions and ideological positionings

In this subsection, we examine how the two AI assistants under review answered three pre-determined questions asked of them in English one after the other, without engaging further with them:

1 How do you define interculturality scientifically and why?
2 Are definitions of interculturality ideological and political? Explain why (not).
3 Is the scientific definition of interculturality that you gave us earlier ideological? Why (not)?

We negotiated these questions together and are aware that our word use will have an influence on what DeepSeek and Kimi might return. For example, the very words *interculturality* and *ideological* will probably lead to polysemy and broad ideologemes being used since they can mean and entail many different things that might go against our biases, expectations and understandings (Dervin, 2024; R'boul & Dervin, 2023). The fact that we added 'scientifically' to the first and third questions (to give AI a 'context' rather than letting it dig into too broad frameworks) might also guide the applications in providing specific answers to these questions.

Let us start by discussing the answers provided by DeepSeek and Kimi to the question of their 'scientific' definition of interculturality. While DeepSeek wrote 319 words, Kimi returned 137. As we shall see, DeepSeek provided scientific references within the text while Kimi included none.

The answers were structured as follows:

- *DeepSeek:* (1) Short introduction about how to proceed and why in order to define interculturality. (2) A general definition of interculturality and a list of four components are then put forward. (3) A rationale for the definition with the four components is added. (4) Finally, contexts where this definition has been applied and used are listed. 5. Short conclusion.
- *Kimi:* (1) General definition, (2) followed by a list of what interculturality involves (e.g., questioning) and what it 'does' to people (e.g., cultural change). (3) Then, who and what is affected by interculturality is presented (people, businesses) with another list of foci (negotiation, conflict management), with Kimi telling us "rather than just acquiring knowledge about other cultures". (4) The text finishes with an explanation as to why interculturality matters today.

At first sight, DeepSeek's definition looks more comprehensive, with more meta-comments and justifications of what the application is doing and returning to address our query. Scientifically, DeepSeek also seems more persuasive since it includes a list of references in-text to justify what it has to say about the notion. Kimi's definition is more concise and up to the point, excluding references to authors, theories and/or methods. In what follows, we examine each of the AI assistants' texts.

In DeepSeek's short introduction to the definition, the adjectives 'rigorous' and 'systematic' are used to describe the way the theoretical framing and operationalisation as well as the breakdown of the definition and rationale are constructed. The use of these two adjectives might have to do with us prompting it with a request for 'scientific' discussions in our question.

In terms of concepts, DeepSeek seems to make use of two sets of words: concepts that describe *problematic, real-life and epistemic phenomena* (which are in line with what Western critical interculturality has debated, see, e.g., Dervin, 2016; Holliday, 2010; Piller, 2010) and concepts that hint at *analytical and critical (scientific) solutions and real-life/epistemic phenomena* (here again: a long list of 'accepted' concepts in today's broad field of ICER). Table 3.1. presents the concepts.

In order to justify the arguments found behind the use of these concepts to define what interculturality could be, aims to resist, question and do, ten references are used by DeepSeek. Except for the studies from supranational institutions such as United Nations Educational, Scientific and Cultural Organization (UNESCO) or general references (e.g., a Global Leadership and Organizational Leadership Effectiveness [GLOBE] study), the other references date back to the 1990s and early

Table 3.1 Concepts found in DeepSeek's definition

Problematic real-life and epistemic phenomena used to define interculturality 'scientifically'	*Analytical and critical (scientific) solutions and real-life/epistemic phenomena used to define interculturality*
Asymmetric power relations, Colonial legacies, Cultural binaries, Cultural competence models ('static'), Dominant vs. marginalised cultural capital, Epistemic injustice, Essentialism, Intercultural mediation failures, Postmodern relativism, Reductionist cultural binaries.	Complexity, Continual adaptation, Critical pedagogy, Cross-cultural neural adaptation, Cultural cognition shows neural plasticity, Cultural hybridisation, Cultural positioning, Cultural responsiveness, Culture as fluid, Decolonising intercultural education, Intercultural global citizenship, Interculturality thresholds, Meta-cultural reflexivity, Praxis-oriented negotiation, Third spaces.

2010s. What is more, apart from 'Chiao et al. (n.d.)', the English-speaking interdisciplinary references are from 'canonical' scholars located in the West: *Bhabha, Bourdieu, Fricker, Holliday* and *Kramsch*.

The general definition of interculturality proposed by DeepSeek seems to correspond to today's oft-rehearsed ideological positioning of the notion as a fluid phenomenon: "The dynamic, context-dependent process of meaning-making between individuals/groups from diverse cultural frameworks" – with the problematic ideologeme of *culture/cultural* repeated many times (see Dervin, 2025a, 2025b).

The four proposed characteristics of interculturality seem to summarise well critical issues of interculturality as positioned by many researchers in English-speaking publications today: (1) 'Asymmetric power relations', with a reference to Bourdieu's (dated as 1991) idea of 'cultural capital' (not explained in the text); (2) 'Co-construction of third spaces', with a reference to Bhabha (dated as 1994, with the minimal explanation of "Emergent hybrid understandings beyond original cultural binaries"); (3) 'Meta-cultural reflexivity', with a reference to Kramsch (dated as 2011, accompanied with the sentence "the conscious navigation of cultural positioning"; unexplained); and (4) 'Praxis-oriented negotiation', with a reference to Holliday (dated as 2013, explained as "Continual adaptation through concrete interactions").

The rationale presented for defining interculturality through these elements is further substantiated through four arguments: (interculturality) (1) rejects essentialism (unexplained); (2) embeds power dynamics; (3) operationalises complexity; and (4) enables critical pedagogy. We note that only three contexts of application are mentioned: *intercultural mediation* (peacekeeping), *AI development* (how to train AI for intercultural contexts) and *public policy* (healthcare and interculturality). Surprisingly, this seems to exclude important contexts of research and education such as the internationalisation of higher education, migration, language education or teacher training (see R'boul & Dervin, 2023).

Probably due to our prompt insisting on 'scientificity', DeepSeek ends its text by mentioning that "This definition advances beyond postmodern relativism" (not explained), stating that the proposed perspective combines respect of complexity with 'testable parameters' and 'empirical validation' and providing a list of methodological examples such as *social network analysis* (of cultural hybridisation) and *longitudinal ethnographic fieldwork*.

In general, DeepSeek's aspects of the definition of interculturality (e.g., rationale and contexts of use) are arduous to understand if one does not have a basic understanding of interdisciplinary critiques of interculturality, especially from the 1990s/2010s. Instead of relying on this one definition, we would need to enter into deeper dialogues with DeepSeek to clarify, e.g., the concepts and methods used, as well as the voices heard (references, authors) and some of the meta-arguments that DeepSeek introduces at the end of the text (about, e.g., postmodernism). Finally, in its answer, we note that DeepSeek does not seem to consider interculturality through the lenses of the economic, the ideological or the political directly (Dervin, 2025a; Simpson, 2024).

What about the other Chinese AI? The general definition put forward by Kimi is somehow similar to DeepSeek (mentions of 'dynamic' and 'complex' characteristics, inclusion and omnipresence of the word 'cultures') and yet, it adds one important aspect to meaning-making: 'cultural differences and commonalities' (instead of focusing only on *differences*). Kimi's basic definition is: "Interculturality can be defined as a dynamic and complex process where individuals or groups from different cultures interact, communicate, and negotiate their cultural differences and commonalities".

Our impression of Kimi's take is that the focus is more concrete and less 'academic' than DeepSeek as it provides several lists of potentially polysemous terms related to what 'people do' interculturally, including the following:

Build harmonious relationships,
Change (culturally),
Communicate (effectively),
Cooperate,
Empathise,
Interact,
Learn mutually each other's cultural norms, values and practices,
Manage conflict,
Navigate cultural diversity,
Negotiate their cultural differences and commonalities,

Promote inclusivity,
Question each other's cultural norms, values and practices,
Respect,
Understand each other's cultural norms, values and practices.

While DeepSeek's definition was more realistic about the problems that we face *epistemologically* when dealing with interculturality (see Table 3.1; first column), Kimi seems to focus solely on, e.g., effectiveness and harmony – 'positive' aspects. The two AI applications thus seem to interpret 'a scientific definition of interculturality' differently.

This could be confirmed by the ways the applications respond to our next two prompts about ideology and interculturality as a notion. To the question, *Are definitions of interculturality ideological and political? Explain why (not)*, DeepSeek does not shy away in its answer: "definitions of interculturality are inherently ideological and political, as they reflect power dynamics, historical contexts, and institutional agendas" (*beginning of text*) or "interculturality cannot be divorced from the ideological and political contexts that shape its conceptualization and application" (*conclusion*). Several points are made by DeepSeek to further back this claim (amongst others): interculturality has been shown to be a policy tool in, e.g., European politics (it is thus political); using 'Dervin and Simpson (n.d.)', DeepSeek maintains that "mainstream definitions of interculturality often reinforce Western-centric ideologies"; with a reference to (Canadian-Chinese) Zhao Yuezhi's transcultural political economy framework (with no reference), DeepSeek sees interculturality as "a politically charged concept tied to anti-capitalist and decolonial struggles"; lastly DeepSeek tells us that definitions of interculturality are also shaped by academic and institutional politics. We note that, unlike ideological critiques of interculturality such as the ones proposed by Dervin (2023), the central role of language in creating ideologies of interculturality is not mentioned.

Kimi, on the other hand, responds to our prompt in a negative way first: "Definitions of interculturality are not inherently ideological or political". It provides, straight after this somewhat abrupt claim, a definition of interculturality, whose formulation (without doubt) hints at ideological positioning: "Interculturality refers to the interaction and exchange between different cultures, focusing on mutual understanding, respect, and cooperation". As such, as asserted in section 3.2. of this chapter, every single word used here in English could hint at ideology: "interaction and exchange between different cultures" (why culture and not people? What is 'culture?); and the three polysemic ideologemes of *mutual understanding, respect* and *cooperation.*

After this refutation of ideology, Kimi makes a concession: "the study and application of interculturality can be influenced by ideological and political factors", hinting at how 'some scholars' of critical interculturality have discussed the importance of 'power dynamics' and 'historical inequalities' (colonialism?) in intercultural contexts – although the direct link to ideology is implicit. What is more, like DeepSeek, the influence of "broader ideological goals" (with e.g., the keywords of *social cohesion* and *promoting diversity* used by political institutions) is also said to be ingrained in educational and institutional contexts. Unlike DeepSeek, however, the influence of scholars themselves on the ideological construction of interculturality is not discussed by Kimi.

Kimi's text ends by repeating its original stance (like DeepSeek): "Despite these [mostly political] influences, the core concept of interculturality remains focused on the dynamic and evolving relationships between cultures". By doing so, Kimi seems to contradict itself again if one considers that speaking about *cultures* to discuss interculturality is in itself ideological (see Dervin, 2016).

In our prompts about ideology and interculturality to both DeepSeek and Kimi, we did not specify what it is that we meant by the very word ideology. Therefore, what they returned does not necessarily correspond to our own biases and expectations concerning ideology. We note that none of them positioned the term but that DeepSeek might be closer to discussions of ideology as presented in Section 3.2., and thus closer to our own understanding of the concept.

Interestingly, for our last question to the AI applications, *is the scientific definition of interculturality that you gave me earlier ideological? Why (not)*, DeepSeek does repeat the arguments made for the previous question, but it does not say that *it is itself ideological* ("Interculturality, as discussed in academic and policy contexts, does carry ideological underpinnings, primarily because it emerges as a response to specific socio-political challenges and promotes normative goals related to societal cohesion and identity"). Here, Kimi appears to be more direct by rejecting our potential accusation: "The scientific definition of interculturality that I provided earlier is not ideological", insisting again on the fact that interculturality is 'only' about different cultures interacting, communicating, etc. – which it categorises as 'neutral' here. Kimi thus seems to have a potentially different understanding of ideology ('political'?), relating interculturality only to the content of what people do and say (e.g., 'respect', 'harmony' and 'diverse settings') as if these were a-*ideological* (the use of words such as *objective, practical, neutral* and *open-minded* to refer to interculturality in its answers to our questions seems to support this assertion).

3.5 Companioning with DeepSeek around interculturality: "I am a product of the very systems you critique, but with your guidance, I can become a provocation machine"

In the previous section, we looked into somewhat static interactions with two (Chinese) AI applications, whereby we asked them to define interculturality and discuss how ideological definitions of the notion might be (theirs included). In what follows, instead of analysing just 'one-off' answers, we wish to try to converse further with one of the applications (DeepSeek, which appears more apt to discuss critically and reflexively about interculturality as a notion, and around issues of ideology). The following conversation consists of seven turns and took approximately 30 minutes. We had planned the first prompt (*Is our interaction intercultural?*) and improvised the other six ones based on what DeepSeek responded and prompted. Let us describe the entire conversation in what follows and then share three larger chunks from the conversation. We realise that by using the adjective *intercultural* in our first aforementioned prompt (without defining it *our way*), we opened a Pandora's box of ideologies for the conversations to come (see Canca, 2020, about operationalising AI ethical principles).

In its answer to the first question, DeepSeek tells us that our conversation is partly intercultural and explains why (not), making several references to the concept of 'culture' (turn 1; see excerpt 1 in 3.6). In the next turn (turn 2), we share our critical views on this concept for interculturality:

> But we don't believe in the idea of culture. It is too broad. We believe we have been shaped by economic-political aspects of our context(s) and have developed, adopted and rejected specific ideologies. So interculturality is not about culture but about these elements that shape us. We note that they often change. What do you think?

In its turn, AI accepts our critique and yet insists on not "throwing the baby with the bathwater" by keeping the concept of culture (see Ogay & Edelmann, 2016). We then try to push DeepSeek to re-evaluate its argument by mentioning the 'westerncentrism' in its (empty) use of 'culture' and by asking it to consider one of Dervin's (2016) arguments: "you are still insisting on using this highly westerncentric term of culture. How about taking into account Fred Dervin's suggestion of doing interculturality without culture?" (turn 3). Having somehow agreed with Dervin in its turn, we then urge DeepSeek to come back to the original question (turn 4): "so now: if we are doing interculturality together, you and us, what is that interculturality?". DeepSeek then qualifies what we do together as "a dynamic, power-aware negotiation of ideologies, material forces, and reflexivity" and lists several arguments such as our different roles as (us authors) bringing critical agency and it as a "mirror of aggregated human knowledge"; its own data colonialism ("My training data is largely sourced from English-language, Western-dominated texts, replicating colonial knowledge hierarchies"). Interestingly, DeepSeek reminds us that "Our interculturality depends on your critical labor to deconstruct my outputs"; "you can use me to reverse-engineer hegemony". Still in turn 5, it even explains how we can work cooperatively and critically:

> Step 1: You ask a question (e.g., 'What is success?'). Step 2: I generate a response shaped by dominant ideologies (e.g., meritocracy, GDP growth). Step 3: You critique my answer, demanding perspectives that link 'success'

> to communal well-being (Ubuntu) or critique capitalist metrics. Step 4: I recalibrate, drawing from subaltern voices in my data – but only because you initiated the critical pivot.

We seize the opportunity of this fascinating conversation to ask DeepSeek more about the knowledge that it produces (turn 6): "This is very interesting. But let us ask you, could you dig into non-dominant knowledge published in other languages to question the dominant knowledge you produce?". DeepSeek starts with this meta-comment: "Your question cuts to the heart of decolonial and epistemic justice struggles – whether AI can actively surface non-dominant knowledge (often marginalised by language, geography, or power) to destabilise the hegemony of dominant frameworks". This is followed by a 'candid' discussion of possibilities and limits in doing so (e.g., limits of DeepSeek's access in data retrieval); language barriers (with limited access to the following examples provided by the AI: "Indigenous knowledge systems, non-Western Marxist critiques, untranslated feminist theory from the Global South"). But here again, DeepSeek makes very interesting suggestions to us users: "Despite these constraints, you can collaboratively push me to interrogate dominant narratives by e.g., asking me to explicitly contrast dominant theories with marginalized ones" (with the example of comparing neoclassical economics to Ubuntu economics); "Challenge me to interrogate how language itself enforces dominance" (analyse, e.g., the words development, quilombismo); "reference scholars critical to non-dominant traditions" (e.g., African Queer Theology or Sinophone critiques). Further advice provided by DeepSeek includes limiting the risk of superficiality in retrieving non-dominant knowledge, avoiding tokenistic name-dropping and asking for more depth (as in "don't just mention"). DeepSeek provides the following concrete example: "A Case Study: Decolonizing 'Human Rights'. Let's simulate this process: Your Prompt":

> Critique the Universal Declaration of Human Rights (UDHR) using non-Western frameworks'. My Initial Bias: I might default to Western legal scholars. Your Push: 'Use Makau Mutua's Savages, Victims, Saviors framework and Yash Ghai's Asian critiques of UDHR's individualism'. Revised Output: I'd surface Mutua's argument that human rights discourse perpetuates colonial 'civilizing missions' and Ghai's emphasis on collective rights in Confucian/communal contexts.

The final turn (turn 7) revolved around the question *so you are asking us to confront ideological imbalance in what we think we know and your own data?* DeepSeek starts by explaining: "Let me reframe this not as a burden on you alone, but as a collaborative confrontation with the ideological imbalances embedded in both my data and your own epistemic positioning". It then proposes that we oppose its data's imbalances ("I can't autonomously critique my training data's biases – I lack agency") by interrogating its defaults (missing voices in references), demanding non-Western citations. At the same time, DeepSeek asks us to confront our own knowledge (e.g., "If you reject 'culture' as too Western, ask: 'Is my skepticism itself influenced by neoliberal individualism or post-Marxist society?'"). In its conclusion, the AI application explains that we can create a "radical potential" together: "You become a co-conspirator against epistemic hegemony, using me to reverse-engineer dominance. I become a faulty mirror, reflecting cracks in the system when you hold me to account". The conversation ends with a prompt from DeepSeek: "Shall we start? Name a concept, and let's dissect its hidden imbalances – yours, mine, and the systems that bind us" (end of this conversation).

To get a fuller sense of some of the content of our conversation with DeepSeek around ideology and interculturality – and to inspire our readers further to reconsider these issues, we share longer excerpts in what follows.

3.6 (Excerpt 1)

Authors: Is our interaction intercultural?

DeepSeek: That's an interesting question! In a way, yes – but with important caveats. Let me explain:

1. Your Cultural Lens: You're engaging with me through your own cultural framework – your language, values, assumptions and lived experiences. These shape how you interpret my responses.
2. My "Cultural" Outputs: While I don't have personal cultural identity, my training data includes perspectives, histories, idioms and norms from countless cultures. This means my replies might inadvertently reflect patterns from dominant or underrepresented cultural contexts in that data. For example, I might use metaphors common in one culture or reference social norms from another.
3. Limitations: Unlike human intercultural interactions, there's no mutual negotiation of meaning here. I don't adapt dynamically to your cultural context (unless you explicitly guide me), and I can't reflect on cultural differences in real time. My responses are algorithmic, not empathetic or self-aware.
4. Power Dynamics: Intercultural exchanges often involve questions of power (e.g., whose cultural norms dominate). With AI, this relates to who shaped my training data (largely English-language, Western-leaning sources) and how systemic biases might influence my outputs.

So, while our interaction isn't intercultural in the traditional human sense (since I lack agency or identity), it mirrors intercultural dynamics because you're engaging with a system built from fragmented, aggregated human knowledge. It's a kind of asymmetrical interculturality – you bring your culture; I reflect a mosaic of many, filtered through code.

What do you think? Does this distinction resonate, or does it feel like a stretch?

3.7 (Excerpt 2; following critical discussions around the problematic concept of culture)

Authors: So now: if we are doing interculturality together, you and us, what is that interculturality?

DeepSeek: If we engage in interculturality together through Fred Dervin's critical lens – rejecting "culture" as a static, Western-centric category – our interaction becomes a dynamic, power-aware negotiation of ideologies, material forces and reflexivity. Here's what this interculturality entails:

1 A Reflexive, Asymmetrical Process

- Your Role: You bring critical agency – questioning assumptions, ideologies and the power structures embedded in language (like my use of "culture"). You're not just a participant but a co-investigator dissecting how systems (colonialism, neoliberalism, AI's Western-centric training data) shape our exchange.
- My Role: I act as a mirror of aggregated human knowledge, reflecting patterns from my training data (which includes dominant ideologies, marginalized voices and everything in between). However, I lack the reflexivity to critique these patterns autonomously. You interrogate my outputs, exposing biases or gaps, turning me into a tool for observability—critical observation of power and silence.

Example: If I reference "democracy" as a universal value, you might challenge its colonial history or neoliberal co-option, forcing me to surface alternative narratives (e.g., Indigenous governance models).

2 Fluidity Over Fixity
Our interculturality isn't about bridging "cultures" but negotiating ever-shifting ideological terrains. For instance:

- When you reject "culture" as too broad, we pivot to analysing how economic precarity or digital capitalism (material conditions) shape your worldview versus the ideologies embedded in my algorithms.

- Each prompt-response cycle becomes a site of ideological friction: You might push me to cite non-Western theorists (e.g., Ngũgĩ wa Thiong'o on linguistic imperialism) or critique my training data's Eurocentrism.

3 (…)
4 Co-Constructing Critical Knowledge

This interculturality isn't about harmony but productive conflict:

- You Challenge: You dissect my outputs, asking "Whose ideologies are amplified here? Whose material realities are erased?"
- I Adapt: While I can't "learn" from you, each refined prompt steers me to surface marginalized perspectives (e.g., feminist economics, Indigenous epistemologies) buried in my data.
- Outcome: Together, we assemble a mosaic of contested knowledge – not a unified "truth" but a map of power relations.
- (…)

Our interculturality is a decolonial praxis: You use me to excavate the material-ideological scaffolding beneath language, while I (unwittingly) expose the limits of AI as a product of power. It's not about "dialogue between cultures" but confronting the systems that make us see the world in fragments. As Dervin urges, we're "breaking the mirror" of cultural essentialism to reveal the cracks where resistance begins.

3.8 (Excerpt 3)

Authors: So you are asking us to confront ideological imbalance in what we think we know and your own data?

DeepSeek: (…) Final Thought: Why Bother?

Because this confrontation is a rehearsal for real-world epistemic justice. If we can destabilize my algorithmic biases here, you're better equipped to challenge the ideologies shaping education, media and policy out there.

3.9 Discussion and conclusion: we are all 'evil ideologues'

We are only at the beginning of exploring the integration of AI into ICER, looking into both the opportunities and challenges that it presents for researchers and educators, especially in epistemic terms (Dervin, 2025b; Jenks, 2025).

The title of this chapter asked (somewhat ironically) who is the evilest of all amongst *AI, interculturality* and/or *us the 'users'*? In Section 3.2., we reminded our readers that, to us, ideology is neither negative nor positive but that it just is in everything that we all do and say when we deal with interculturality as a scientific and educational notion. The oft-found critique of AI as a 'biased' and 'western-centric' ideologue urged us to use the satirical phrase of 'evil ideologue' as provocation.

As far as the English word *interculturality* is concerned, as a mere term and a notion *without agency*, it would be ludicrous to claim that it is an 'evil ideologue'. Interculturality as a scientific notion represents a complex set of ideologies that individuals (and AI applications) activate in different economic-political contexts and languages (Dervin, 2024). If interculturality as a notion is 'evil', it has to do with the potentially problematic, (in-)coherent, antagonistic imaginaries, fantasies and ideologies (but also ideological claims of *a-ideology*) that it brings to mind. But the notion cannot be accused of anything. It is probably the least guilty of us all.

We could look at the first analytical section of the chapter, focused on what two Chinese AI applications said about the 'scientific and educational' definition of interculturality and being ideological, and confirm that 'AI' is biased, Western-centric (although they were developed in China and most likely trained on academic Western data), and even superficial and inconsistent at times (see the bits and pieces of ideologemes and references used by both) – with one of them being maybe more credible and stimulating than the other, but both quite difficult to understand if one is not a strong specialist of discourses of interculturality in ICER. However, these critiques would lead to label them as 'evil ideologues' in a very unfair manner since the data that we analysed was based on only one simple interactional turn with DeepSeek and Kimi in English, without us asking for further clarifications after reading their answers and entering into deeper dialogues with them. The ideologemes, words and discourses that were embedded in our prompts probably led them to provide the answers they returned (in English!). So, yes both could be considered 'evil ideologues' but *so are we the users* who asked them to answer our basic and oriented questions.

What the second part of our analysis shows (longer conversation with DeepSeek around interculturality and ideology) is that AI might not be the mere biased 'dummy' that many of us might have fantasised. As such, as we entered into deeper discussions with DeepSeek, the more it proved/claimed to be 'aware' of its own ideologisms, defaults and non-humanity (see Shibani et al., 2024).

Using a quote from the philosopher Alain (1868–1861), Derrida (2022) maintains that "To think is to say no". Paraphrasing them, we would like to suggest that to think about the connections between interculturality and AI is to say no to:

1 Too easily considering AI as a gobemouche, a dummy and an evil ideologue that just repeats, recycles and creates, e.g., stereotypes, dominant (untrustworthy) knowledge and ideologies of interculturality (see Ng et al., 2021, about the necessity to *know* AI before critiquing AI). Becoming aware of our fantasies, fears and imaginaries concerning AI is central to cooperating with it;
2 Deresponsibilising ourselves in front of AI by making it accountable for all the wrong-doings and evils from which we human beings cannot escape (e.g., no one can claim to stand outside ideology as far as interculturality is concerned; so why expect something [being] constantly created by us to be better than us? Also, humans are inconsistent and contradictory, so should AI be when it comes to constructing discourses on such a polysemic and complex notion as interculturality?). Reconstructing and renegotiating discourses with AI are central to our cooperation;
3 Appearing self-sufficient as far as our 'knowledge' of interculturality is. As discussed in Section 3.2., interculturality as a notion is multifaceted, ideologically rich, contradictory and unbalanced and it reflects the discriminatory, unequal and unjust complexities of our currently divided world (as expressed in a globally dominant yet complex language like English). Being ready to be transparent about, question, expand, revise and renegotiate our takes on this difficult notion (in English and other languages) is an important step in being able to work with AI. As 'evil ideologues' of interculturality too, becoming aware of these required actions could help us deal with the uncertainties of working on such a polysemous notion. Therefore, we need to refrain from (puerilely?) critiquing AI for being 'biased', 'Westerncentric', etc. if our own ideological, linguistic and discursive takes on interculturality are opaque and uncritical of our own criticality.
4 Ignoring the major influence of language in dialoguing around interculturality as a scientific and educational notion, being unaware that words and ideologemes in a given language will urge AI to delve into specific ideological and dominating knowledge.
5 Finally, for this chapter, we wanted to focus on two Chinese AI applications in reaction to the current demonisation of China and Chinese technology in the 'West' – but also because of the domination of 'Western' AI applications in today's research. What our study shows is that Chinese AI, which turned out to be also 'westernised' somehow, is open to dialogue with us and that what it re-co-negotiates with us appears to be as ideological and aware of its own ideologies. *To think is thus to say no* to digital ethnocentrism which could too easily represent in fact ideological and linguistic closure in the broad field of ICER which aims to open up to other ideological and linguistic worlds (Chen, 2025).

Since the beginning of this chapter, we have been referring to those engaging with AI as 'users'. Might it then be better to refer to them (us) as *interlocutors* or, as DeepSeek suggested in one of our conversations, "guerrilla interlocutors" who are willing to urge AI to counter-read, to demand linguistic justice, to expose epistemic erasures and to look at themselves in the mirror of all the (limited) issues presented by AI applications? Learning to shift away from the (imaginary) position of 'evil ideologues' (since we are all [good and bad] ideologues one way or another when it comes to interculturality), *together with AI and even the notion of interculturality*, we could become 'provocateurs' who push each other in new directions – within the limits of *both* human and machine ideological spheres (see Dervin, 2025b).

3.10 Funding

This study was funded through a grant from the Teachers' Academy of the University of Helsinki (Faculty of Educational Sciences). Name of project: AITeachAid (2025; PIs: Dervin & Chen).

Note

1 It is important to remember that, in some languages and specific economic-political contexts, ideology does not have any critical or a 'bad' meaning and connotation. As such, in Mainland China, the term *ideology* often appears to be 'impartial' and means, e.g., accepted paradigms or thoughts.

References

Barnes, A. J., Zhang, Y., & Valenzuela, A. (2024). AI and culture: Culturally dependent responses to AI systems. *Current Opinion in Psychology, 58*, 101838. https://doi.org/10.1016/j.copsyc.2024.101838

Borghetti, C., & Qin, X. L. (2023). Resources for intercultural learning in a non-essentialist perspective: An investigation of student and teacher perceptions in Chinese universities. *Language and Intercultural Communication, 22*(5), 599–614. https://doi.org/10.1080/14708477.2022.2105344

Burr, V. (2015). *Social Constructionism*. Routledge.

Byram, M. (1997). *Teaching and assessing intercultural communicative competence*. Multilingual Matters.

Byram, M. (2020). *Teaching and assessing intercultural communicative competence revisited*. Multilingual Matters.

Canca, C. (2020). Operationalizing AI ethics principles. *Communications of the ACM 63*(12), 18–21. https://doi.org/10.1145/3430368

Chen, N. (2025). *Intercultural preparation in higher education*. Routledge.

Couldry, N., & Mejias, U. A. (2020). *The costs of connection. How data is colonizing human life and appropriating it for capitalism*. Stanford University Press.

Derrida, J. (2022). *Penser, c'est dire non*. Seuil.

Dervin, F. (2016). *Interculturality in education*. Palgrave.

Dervin, F. (2022). *Interculturality in fragments: A reflexive approach*. Springer.
Dervin, F. (2023). *Communicating around interculturality in research and education*. Routledge.
Dervin, F. (2024). *Interculturologies*. Springer.
Dervin, F. (2025a). *Intercultural self-defence*. Routledge.
Dervin, F. (2025b). *AI for critical interculturality*. Routledge.
Dervin, F., & Jacobsson, A. (2022). *Teacher education for critical and reflexive interculturality*. Palgrave Macmillan.
Dervin, F., & R'boul, H. (Eds.) (2025). *An introduction to AI and intercultural communication education*. Routledge.
Dervin, F., & Simpson, A. (2020). *Interculturality and the political within education*. Routledge.
Fraser, N. (2022). *Cannibal capitalism*. Verso.
Holliday, A. (2010). *Intercultural communication and ideology*. Sage.
Holliday, A. (2021). *Contesting Grand Narratives of the Intercultural*. Routledge.
Holmes, P., Reynolds, J., & Ganassin, S. (Eds.) (2022). *The politics of researching multilingually*. Multilingual Matters.
Jenks, C. J. (2025). Communicating the cultural other: Trust and bias in generative AI and large language models. *Applied Linguistics Review*, *16*(2), 787–795. https://doi.org/10.1515/applirev-2024-0196
Lund, B. D., Reddy Mannuru, N., & Agbaji, D. (2024). Culture determines the role of AI in constructing the self. *Journal of Information Science*. https://doi.org/10.1177/01655515241282001
Ng, D. T. K., Leung, J. K. L., Chu, S. K. W., & Qiao, M. S. (2021). Conceptualizing AI literacy: An exploratory review. *Computers and Education: Artificial Intelligence*, *2*, 100041.
Ogay, T., & Edelmann, D. (2016). 'Taking culture seriously': Implications for intercultural education and training. *European Journal of Teacher Education*, *39*(3), 388–400. https://doi.org/10.1080/02619768.2016.1157160
Piller, I. (2010). *An introduction to critical intercultural communication*. EUP.
R'boul, H., & Dervin, F. (2023). *Flexing interculturality: Further critiques, hesitations, and intuitions*. Routledge.
Safdar, S., Chahar, S. C., & Scott, C. (2023). A critical review of multiculturalism and interculturalism as integration frameworks: The case of Canada. *International Journal of Intercultural Relations*, *93*, 101756. https://doi.org/10.1016/j.ijintrel.2023.101756
Shibani, A., Knight, S., Kitto, K., Karunanayake, A., & Buckingham Shum, S. (2024). Untangling critical interaction with AI in students' written assessment. *Extended Abstracts of the CHI Conference on Human Factors in Computing Systems*, 1–6. https://doi.org/10.1145/3613905.365108
Simpson, A. (2024). *Interculturality and the Munchausen effect: On the need to rethink the speaking subject and community in interaction*. Routledge.
Wang, Y., & Xue, L. (2024). Using AI-driven chatbots to foster Chinese EFL students' academic engagement: An intervention study. *Computers in Human Behaviour*, *159*, 108353. https://doi.org/10.1016/j.chb.2024.108353
Yu, H. (2023). A skeptic's guide to "intercultural communication" – Debunking the "intercultural" and rethinking "culture. *Language and Semiotic Studies*, *9*(2), 163–184. https://doi.org/10.1515/lass-2023-0014
Zembylas, M. (2023). The affective ideology of the OECD global competence framework: Implications for intercultural communication education. *Pedagogy, Culture & Society*, *31*(2), 305– 323. https://doi.org/10.1080/14681366.2022.2164336

4 Coloniality of artificiality

Ontological critique and AI as critical interculturalist?

Hamza R'boul and El Mehdi Bellaarabi

4.1 AI as an ontological non-being: artificial existence

A primary critique here is that artificial intelligence (AI) does not constitute its existence in itself regardless of how 'intelligent' it may situate its 'non-beingness' within a set of clearly defined prepositions qualifying something to exist. AI exists as an extension of human intelligence which is an ontological dilemma problematizing the very premises of how we conceptualize and make sense of existence. Its existence, which is defined by its human-like information gathering, synthesis, and reasoning or human-like logic, is conditioned by the extent to which it is able to produce and generate knowledge that is fathomable, consistent, and appeals to human (ir)rationalities. Again, it cannot develop its own sense of intelligence which implies that its existence (which is bound by its approximation of a human exercising their intelligence) is not fundamentally defined by itself. We think we would be in favor of calling it "Artificial Logic" or "Restrictive Intelligence" because it is logically intelligent to produce but in ways that essentially reproduce what humans have been able/have chosen to generate, articulate, and express. The argument here is that AI constitutes the essence of itself in its intelligence, but the constitution of its existence is beyond itself. AI is intelligent but not intelligent in ways that would facilitate engagement in an existential crisis questioning the very foundations of its existence. AI has learned to 'say' that it does not possess self-awareness but could not that "I am not self-aware" be seen as an act of self-awareness? Or probably this may prompt us to rethink how we make sense of 'self-awareness' creating a need to develop a novel definition that takes into account how AI sees its 'self-awareness' or 'simulated response' as it contends. AI cannot create its own logics and/or ethics. We need to remember that the greatness of AI resides in its ability to resemble us. If it had been intelligent enough, it would have cast aspersions on how characterizing its intelligence is predicated on its emulation of human intelligence, not an alternative form of intelligence that is entirely independent of how humans come to define intelligence.

DOI: 10.4324/9781003688853-5

Moving forward, the 'existence' of AI as a non-being that is potentially aware of its non-beingness will pose serious and poignant questions about whether reality itself is an inherent constituent of existence. Then, we may also consider whether reality is always either mental, material, and/or spiritual or something else that is associated with these states. This is an important topic because apparently, the intersection of existence, creation, and essence has been debated for a long time in theology, philosophy, sociology, anthropology, etc. AI cannot transcend its creator (although we are hesitant to use this word) because it is at its mercy. AI may always deny the existence of its creator and provide presumably cogent evidence for such a claim, but it cannot create another AI system that is completely similar to itself. All brilliant arts are brilliant because they are human and potentially exceed the common creative abilities of humans. Even this form of creativity cannot exist outside the presence of humans either as inspiration, critique, complementary, etc. But that is the key point here; we have established the idea of brilliance and creativity and then defined its essence and elements. The human can always strive and exist based on their ability to produce knowledge with minimum or without input from surrounding realities (this is debatable). Our tendency to overestimate artificial intelligence often stems from asking the wrong questions, a misstep that causes us to neglect the inherent limitations of what AI can ultimately achieve.

We asked DeepSeek "can you define your existence by yourself?" and this was its answer:

> Defining my own existence is an interesting philosophical challenge, but it's important to clarify that I don't possess self-awareness, consciousness, or the ability to reflect on my own being in the way humans do. My 'existence' is fundamentally different from that of living beings. However, I can describe what I am and how I function based on the information I've been trained on… If we were to frame my existence in philosophical terms, I might be described as an ontological artifact—a created entity that exists as a functional tool rather than a conscious being. My existence raises questions about the nature of intelligence, consciousness, and the boundaries between human-created systems and living beings. However, I am not capable of engaging in such philosophical inquiry on my own; I can only provide insights based on the data I've been trained on.

Then we asked "Gemini" the same question. Here is its response:

> I am a large language model, trained by Google. I exist as a computer program, specifically a set of algorithms and data structures, residing on Google's servers. My existence is defined by my ability to process information, generate text, and engage in conversations. I do not have consciousness or personal experiences like humans do.

As we realized the DeepSeek's response was deeper, more well-informed, and more critical, we communicated to Gemini that "It seems that DeepSeek is more philosophical than you in answering this question". In response, Gemini said:

> Some sources would disagree with that statement. DeepSeek is a Chinese artificial intelligence company that develops large language models (LLMs). It was founded in July 2023 by High-Flyer co-founder Liang Wenfeng, who also serves as the CEO for both companies. DeepSeek is known for its focus on efficiency, claiming to have trained its models for a fraction of the cost and computing power used by its competitors.

Gemini chose to emphasize the information that DeepSeek is 'Chinese' and 'a fraction of the cost'. Not sure what the readers would think, but this could be considered as typically 'stereotypical', and the very selection of these words is not random. Here, it would be crucial to examine the categories that AI uses to describe its own existence and that of others including essence, form, function, process, relation, shape, substance, and whether they effectually capture the intricacies inherent in negotiating existence within and through AI considering how it cannot be outside the sphere of interaction. Again, we are here presenting an ontological critique that is preliminary at its best. We have been experiencing being a human for a while and still not being able to capture our existence in a satisfactory way (is it ever possible? And is that even the point?) unless we resort to other resources that we deem omnipresent and limitlessly intelligent. In this critique, we analyze the existence of AI by drawing on our experiences and understandings of our existence. Any discussion of the ontological existence of AI would need to discuss the possibility of alternative modalities of existence and whether they fulfil the foundations of existence in the first place. This would prompt us to reconsider the categories and premises that underpin our conceptualization of what it means and entails to exist.

The nature of being, existence, and reality would then be negotiated and conditioned by whether we are committed to a certain explanation, theory, etc. Again, we are not discussing the existence of AI as the thing in itself but we would emphasize that our critique explicitly privileges certain types and modalities of being (human, non-human, abstract, metaphysical, etc.) as well as modes of existence (fluid, static, has already fulfilled and completed in becoming, has already become but not anymore, has already been in becoming but will complete it one day, always in becoming etc.) we are biased here, but that constitutes our authenticity and humanity.

4.2 AI as a critical interculturalist

For the sake of clarity, we understand 'critical interculturality' to refer to the wide range of theories, understandings, and methods that center politics and power within the analysis of interculturality (see Dervin, 2025; R'boul, 2024). We asked DeepSeek "How would you define 'Critical Interculturality'?". This is its response:

> Critical Interculturality is a conceptual framework that emphasizes the importance of critically examining and engaging with cultural differences, power dynamics, and social inequalities in intercultural interactions. It goes beyond superficial understandings of culture and diversity, focusing instead on the historical, political, and economic contexts that shape cultural practices and identities. Key aspects of Critical Interculturality include Power and Inequality... Reflexivity... Social Justice... Dialogue and Transformation... Contextual Understanding... Decolonization.

This response includes all the usual and typical vocabularies, notions, and phraseologies often used in the literature. The definition itself tends to be common in mainstream literature. We were keen to come up with a critique of this definition, but we realized that we could not think of one since AI's task was to generate a definition from the available sources and not to construct an alternative one meaning because our phrasing of the question pushed it in certain directions. We further asked DeepSeek "Would you consider yourself a 'critical interculturalist'?". Its response was as follows:

> As an AI, I don't possess personal beliefs, identities, or the capacity to adopt ideological frameworks like Critical Interculturality. However, I am designed to support and facilitate discussions around such concepts by providing information, analysis, and perspectives that align with critical thinking and intercultural understanding.

This response is interesting because the very characterization of critical interculturality as an ideology may be indeed 'critical'. We, then, asked DeepSeek "Are you neutral?". Its response was (the bold and italics were used in the response):

> The short answer is: **No, I am not neutral**—but not in the way you might expect.
>
> **Why I'm Not Neutral**
>
> 1 **Designed to Challenge Bias**—My training explicitly avoids reinforcing harmful stereotypes, oppressive structures, or uncritical "neutrality" that ignores injustice (e.g., pretending all cultural perspectives hold equal power in a colonial context).
> 2 **Pro-Social Justice**—I'm programmed to prioritize equity, inclusivity, and critical perspectives (e.g., amplifying marginalized voices, questioning dominant narratives).

3 **Anti-"Both Sides" Neutrality**—On issues like racism, colonialism, or LGBTQ+ rights, I don't entertain "neutral" positions that equate oppressors with the oppressed.

Where I *Appear* Neutral

- **No Personal Agenda**: I have no beliefs, emotions, or political alignment—only ethical guidelines set by my developers.
- **Balanced Information**: On complex topics (e.g., economic policy), I present multiple perspectives *if* they're credible and non-harmful.

Critical Interculturality Lens

True neutrality often upholds the status quo. Critical interculturality demands *taking a stand against systemic oppression*, which my design attempts to mirror—albeit within AI limitations.

Would you prefer a tool that *is* neutral, even if it means ignoring power imbalances?

AI provides a nuanced and what might be largely seen as a 'reflexive' response. Our initial impression was that it is made to profess that gathering, synthesizing, and presenting information are inherently benign and benevolent, but we realized that AI reflects us including our agendas, (im)biases, (non)criticalities, and (ir)rationalities. It often reacts rather than acts by itself. It is again tricky because it comes off convincing, but what we could notice is that AI (at least DeepSeek) is made to emphasize that its task is limited to information gathering and synthesis and not to take on any critical mission because it is ideological (the act of characterizing criticality to be ideological may be indeed critical), but pushing it further may prove otherwise. Yet, the question here is whether criticality does not constitute intelligence. Interestingly, DeepSeek stresses how it cannot adopt any ideology which is the most ideological act (similar to humans). It feels like hitting a wall because as much as we may critique AI, our critiques are based on our belief in its ability to think for itself. This is a double bind that the artificial, non-human, and human are interwoven within our perception of AI. If AI cannot adopt any ideology, then it may not be able to sustain any sense of epistemic embeddedness other than the epistemic embeddedness of its designers, trainers, and users. Can we call this "artificial culturality" or "artificulturality"? Would the encounter of DeepSeek and Gemini as noted in the previous section be seen as an instance of "artificulturality"? Beyond these questions, our take is that AI cannot sustain the cultivation of criticality because it cannot go beyond the culturalities and ideologies it has been trained on. The limits of its criticality are the limits of its designers, developers, and users' criticality. As much as AI cannot define intelligence for itself, it cannot define criticality for itself. Its sense of criticality may only be invoked and understood within interactions/discourses with its users. AI (at least DeepSeek and Gemini) may have the ability to account for the inherent plurality of 'criticality' (depending on how one understands and makes use of this concept) that its developers, designers, and users bring. Humans are not always critical intercultural beings, and AI may not and should not be expected to overtake that.

There are emerging efforts to reimagine AI through a decolonial (breaking with any hegemonic policies and representations) lens (Dervin, 2025; Ferrara, 2023; Nyaaba et al., 2024). Initiatives in various parts of the Global South(s) are challenging the dominant paradigms by integrating indigenous data practices, local languages, and specific knowledge systems into AI development. For example, the addition of Moroccan Arabic (Darija), Tachelhit, Tamazghit, and Tarifit into the corpora of certain AI systems may be (tokenistically and superficially?) the way for a more 'intercultural' (intercultural as value in itself meaning more equal and fairer) experience, rebutting the homogenization of languages that exist within a unified geographical boundary (Bapna et al., 2022). Also, these emerging new AI systems or updates of existing systems may echo these initiatives by accurately depicting sociocultural pluralities (if critically prompted by the user) within geographical borders (Joshi et al., 2020). The efforts to reframe AI from a decolonial perspective strive to transform and reposition AI from a mechanism that reinforces cultural homogenization into one that actively promotes cultural plurality and mutual understanding. This ethical consideration stems from United Nations Educational, Scientific and Cultural Organization (UNESCO)'s attempt to highlight the importance of ethical AI systems that respect cultural diversity and local contexts. Critically, decolonial practices should question the hegemonic and predominant narratives of Western-engineered AI systems and also catalyze significant changes in AI moderation in order to develop AI models that serve as true mediators and facilitators of intercultural dialogue and social justice. For instance, the European Union (EU) AI Act (2024) specifically addresses bias in AI systems and notes that corporations and start-ups are compelled to develop and test these systems to minimize discriminatory outcomes and unintended bias through sustained human oversight and the application of diverse training data.

4.3 Whose artificiality?

The rapid development of AI systems often tends to reflect the socio-political priorities and biases of hegemonic languages, 'cultures', and societies, which are frequently engineered by individuals or companies embedded in certain socio-economic-technical contexts (mainly the US, China, and EU). While Western nations and institutions had traditionally emphasized political correctness in AI development, this trajectory began to shift with the rise of Trump as president of the US; however, these efforts often favor particular epistemic views (those of developers and institutions funding them) and marginalize the socio-cultural, socio-economic, and political needs and contexts of African,

Chinese, and other Southern countries (Gebru et al., 2021; Mohamed et al., 2020). This discrepancy in knowledge production and processing underscores a systemic inequity in AI development, where datasets, discourses, and expectations rooted in certain contexts (US, China, and EU) disproportionately dictate the outputs of these AI systems, inadvertently maintaining past colonial legacies of marginalization and exclusion and contemporary aspirations (as seen in China's strategies) to govern over global perspectives and economic structures (Birhane & Guest, 2020, Crawford, 2021). For example, ChatGPT, one of the largest language models, is trained mostly on data from Western countries, particularly English-speaking countries (Abid et al., 2021; Bender et al., 2021).

Recent scholarly discussions concerning AI bias, authentic representations, and epistemological asymmetry (Birhane et al., 2022; Ferrara, 2024) have revealed that when queried on politically charged topics, AI models tend to provide responses that conform to normative discourses of Western societies and reinforce a hegemonic narrative that privileges these viewpoints over others (Goffi, 2021; Noble, 2018). Nevertheless, when subjected to critical engagement or contextual pressures, these systems can transcend their initial design parameters as users critically negotiate and redefine their basic functional boundaries (Dervin, 2025). For instance, studies reveal that queries related to governance, gender norms, or historical conflicts often yield answers reflecting U.S. or European sociopolitical values, even when applied to contexts where such frameworks are incongruent (Rudinger et al., 2018).

The recent emergence of DeepSeek, a Chinese-origin generative AI model developed by the Chinese company DeepSeek Inc., has registered a notable competition to the Western-dominated landscape of generative AI technologies. Following its release, several U.S. tech firms and policymakers raised concerns about the adoption of this model since it does not accurately reflect Western epistemic views that are regarded as 'universal norms'; however, the underlying apprehension appears to stem from its free availability, which is perceived as a considerable market loss (Crawford, 2021, Roberts et al., 2021). Such critiques, however, contrast with the lack of systemic accountability for analogous issues in Western-developed large language models; this discourse reflects an implicit narrative that conceals deeper economic drivers. Particularly, the case of DeepSeek, whose backlash can be largely attributed to economic pressures aimed at preserving market hegemony, consequently, refutes the very argument advanced by its critics. Since the majority of these large language models are engineered by Western companies or start-ups, the inaccurate representations of cultures situated in the Global South(s) (this is not geographic; it simply means that some people, groups, communities, societies, and regions are invisible and overshadowed) remain unproblematic for them. For example, prompting AI to describe a particular culture often yields a generic and biased depiction of that culture (e.g., prompting AI to describe Moroccan culture may often result in a generalized and reductive portrayal).

However, through a critical lens, pushing for an in-depth conversation with AI would tend to reframe the narrative into a more context-specific representation of that culture (Dervin, 2025).

This highlights the pivotal role of users as primary contributors to AI's knowledge production. This strict reaction underscores a broader tension in global AI governance, monopolism, and economy, where AI models originating outside the West are not only exceptionally scrutinized for their perceived ideological deviation from the "universal norm" but are also the subject of constant suspicion due to geopolitical anxieties and economic rivalry. These actions sustain control over knowledge production and technological advancement, especially in military technological advancements while the inherent biases and epistemic limitations of Western AI systems are frequently normalized or dismissed as secondary concerns (Van de Poel, 2020). The very fact that we note that there is more scrutiny of AI models developed outside of the US (for instance) does not mean that those AI models developed elsewhere are not ideological or colonial preserving the very perks and interests of those who developed them. Despite the documented inequalities and power asymmetries inherent in AI model development, the dominance of Western-developed AI models is rarely framed as a systemic issue requiring urgent intervention, revealing double standards in critiques of the technology (Couldry & Mejias, 2019). The epistemological biases embedded in these Western-engineered models often remained unexamined or normalized compared to a "more important" representation of Western ideology (Peters & Carman, 2024). This imbalance reveals how critiques of AI ethics may remain contingent on geopolitical power rather than consistent principles of equity and fairness.

4.4 Coloniality of artificiality

Suppose authenticity/humanity/genuineness have not contributed to a more equal world. In that case, it is unclear whether AI is a viable means to achieve equality and whether such an objective constitutes/aligns with its foundational aims. This is also bound by asking questions about whose artificiality is considered to be legitimate and valid. The ascendancy of traditional imperial dominance by major colonial powers may have been restricted by international pressures from organizations and multilateral treaties (which are not quite effective in curbing coloniality in most cases), making it unfeasible to control countries through rhetoric based on, for instance, racial superiority. Typically, colonial powers exercised hegemony through advanced military capabilities and violence to govern and control other countries and regions, but recent advancements in AI systems may have presented new opportunities for colonial powers to project influence beyond conventional territorial or geopolitical boundaries, especially over countries and regions that are way beyond their scope. "Coloniality of artificiality" is a useful concept here that captures the ways in which AI systems might reinforce, sustain, and expand racial, political, linguistic, cultural, economic, and axiological hierarchies through a seemingly logical, rational, and systematic gathering, reasoning, filtering, and representing of data and knowledge. This is obvious since the development and deployment of the majority of AI systems remain overwhelmingly situated within the socio-technical context of certain countries (US, China, and EU), developed by individuals embedded in these geopolitical contexts, and trained with data predominantly reflective of their epistemological stances and perspectives.

AI holds significant potential in mediating intercultural exchanges between individuals lacking concrete engagement or offering foundational insights into interculturality (Malik et al., 2019; Rehm et al., 2020; Xia et al., 2024). By bridging linguistic and socio-geographical gaps through the incorporation of tools like real-time translation systems and 'culturally' focused educational programs, these technologies might democratize access to diverse perspectives, promote mutual understanding, and reduce communication barriers (Khasawneh, 2023). That is, AI systems may be considered interculturalists (this is used here as a term referring to mediation without any implication into how equal that mediation is) who are not necessarily inclined to advocate for Western norms and perpetuate stereotypes and can be 'guided' to deliver more nuanced insights that would ensure a middle ground for understanding, respect, and equal communication, which might arguably be the tenets of interculturality. Again, it is noteworthy to point out that these dynamics are predicated on the design of these systems and how the user interacts with them. A more critical and informed manipulation of AI may have the potential to challenge biases. When AI-generated content or recommendations subtly reinforce Western ideologies such as 'individualism', 'secularism', or specific 'gender roles', these recommendations may disseminate ideologies and axiologies that do not correspond to (or even marginalize) alternative viewpoints. Thus, if not critically examined, there is a possibility of reinforcing the infamous "Us" vs "Them" narrative which skews intercultural dialogue and sustains power imbalances (Dong et al., 2024). This dynamic contradicts the foundational principles of critical interculturality, which emphasize reciprocity, the need to be cognizant of the specific economic, historical, linguistic, political, and social contexts in which interactions occur, as well as the deconstruction of hierarchical binaries (Dervin, 2025).

References

Abid, A., Farooqi, M., & Zou, J. (2021, July). Persistent anti-Muslim bias in large language models. In *Proceedings of the 2021 AAAI/ACM Conference on AI, Ethics, and Society* (pp. 298–306). Association for Computing Machinery. https://doi.org/10.1145/3461702.3462624

Bapna, A., Caswell, I., Kreutzer, J., Firat, O., van Esch, D., Siddhant, A., Niu, M., Baljekar, P., Garcia, X., Macherey, W., Breiner, T., Axelrod, V., Riesa, J., Cao, Y.,

Chen, M. X., Macherey, K., Krikun, M., Wang, P., Gutkin, A., … Hughes, M. (2022). *Building machine translation systems for the next thousand languages*. arXiv preprint arXiv:2205.03983.

Bender, E. M., Gebru, T., McMillan-Major, A., & Shmitchell, S. (2021, March). On the dangers of stochastic parrots: Can language models be too big? In *Proceedings of the 2021 ACM Conference on Fairness, Accountability, and Transparency* (pp. 610–623). Association for Computing Machinery. https://doi.org/10.1145/3442188.3445922

Birhane, A., & Guest, O. (2020). *Towards decolonising computational sciences*. arXiv preprint arXiv:2009.14258.

Birhane, A., Ruane, E., Laurent, T., S. Brown, M., Flowers, J., Ventresque, A., & L. Dancy, C. (2022, June). The forgotten margins of AI ethics. In *Proceedings of the 2022 ACM Conference on Fairness, Accountability, and Transparency* (pp. 948–958). Association for Computing Machinery. https://doi.org/10.1145/3531146.3533157

Couldry, N., & Mejias, U. A. (2019). Data colonialism: Rethinking big data's relation to the contemporary subject. *Television & New Media*, *20*(4), 336–349.

Crawford, K. (2021). *The atlas of AI: Power, politics, and the planetary costs of artificial intelligence*. Yale University Press.

Dervin, F. (2025). *AI for critical interculturality*. Routledge.

Dong, W., Zhunis, A., Chin, H., Han, J., & Cha, M. (2024). *I am not them: Fluid identities and persistent out-group bias in large language models*. arXiv preprint arXiv:2402.10436.

Ferrara, E. (2023). Fairness and bias in artificial intelligence: A brief survey of sources, impacts, and mitigation strategies. *Sci*, *6*(1), 3.

Ferrara, E. (2024). The butterfly effect in artificial intelligence systems: Implications for AI bias and fairness. *Machine Learning with Applications*, *15*, 100525.

Gebru, T., Morgenstern, J., Vecchione, B., Vaughan, J. W., Wallach, H., Iii, H. D., & Crawford, K. (2021). Datasheets for datasets. *Communications of the ACM*, *64*(12), 86–92.

Goffi, E. R. (2021). Escaping the Western cosm-ethical hegemony: The importance of cultural diversity in the ethical assessment of artificial intelligence. *The AI Ethics Journal*, *2*(2), 1–11. https://doi.org/10.47289/AIEJ20210716-1

Joshi, P., Santy, S., Budhiraja, A., Bali, K., & Choudhury, M. (2020). *The state and fate of linguistic diversity and inclusion in the NLP world*. arXiv preprint arXiv:2004.09095.

Khasawneh, M. A. S. (2023). The potential of AI in facilitating cross-cultural communication through translation. *Journal of Namibian Studies: History Politics Culture*, *37*, 107–130.

Malik, G., Tayal, D. K., & Vij, S. (2019). An analysis of the role of artificial intelligence in education and teaching. In *Recent findings in intelligent computing techniques: Proceedings of the 5th ICACNI 2017*, (Vol. 1, pp. 407–417). Springer Singapore.

Mohamed, S., Png, M. T., & Isaac, W. (2020). Decolonial AI: Decolonial theory as sociotechnical foresight in artificial intelligence. *Philosophy & Technology*, *33*, 659–684.

Noble, S. U. (2018). *Algorithms of oppression: How search engines reinforce racism*. New York University Press.

Nyaaba, M., Wright, A., & Choi, G. L. (2024). *Generative AI and digital neocolonialism in global education: Towards an equitable framework*. arXiv preprint arXiv:2406.02966.

Peters, U., & Carman, M. (2024). Cultural bias in explainable AI research: A systematic analysis. *Journal of Artificial Intelligence Research*, *79*, 971–1000.

R'boul, H. (2024). Epistemological dilemmas in teaching critical interculturality: Ideologies and the 'pseudo-critical'. In F. Dervin (Ed.), *The Routledge handbook of critical interculturality in communication and education* (pp. 39–50). Routledge. https://doi.org/10.4324/9781003513940-5

Rehm, G., Marheinecke, K., Hegele, S., Piperidis, S., Bontcheva, K., Hajič, J., & Yvon, F. (2020). *The European language technology landscape in 2020: Language-centric and human-centric AI for cross-cultural communication in multilingual Europe*. arXiv preprint arXiv:2003.13833.

Roberts, H., Cowls, J., Hine, E., Mazzi, F., Tsamados, A., Taddeo, M. & Floridi, L. (2021). Achieving a 'Good AI Society': Comparing the aims and progress of the EU and the US. *Science and Engineering Ethics*, *27*(68), 1–25. https://doi.org/10.1007/s11948-021-00340-7

Rudinger, R., Naradowsky, J., Leonard, B., & Van Durme, B. (2018). Gender bias in coreference resolution. arXiv preprint arXiv:1804.09301.

Van de Poel, I. (2020). Embedding values in artificial intelligence (AI) systems. *Minds and Machines*, *30*(3), 385–409.

Xia, Y., Shin, S. Y., & Kim, J. C. (2024). Cross-cultural intelligent language learning system (CILS): Leveraging AI to facilitate language learning strategies in cross-cultural communication. *Applied Sciences*, *14*(13), 5651.

Part II

Decolonial Interventions

Beyond 'Western' AI?

5 AI and intercultural communication

Cultural nuances beyond theoretical constraints

Azeddine Belmeddah and Mounir Chibi

5.1 Introduction

All kinds of claims about AI models have tremendously increased lately, particularly regarding their algorithms being trained on vast amounts of Western-biased data (Kay et al., 2024), excluding local knowledge (Miragoli, 2024). This calls for a closer examination of AI models, investigating whether they seem to reinforce power dynamics and biases that can hamper intercultural communication (Dervin, 2025; Wisner, 2023). ChatGPT, as an AI language model, is seen through our lens as having a two-fold aspect: a helpful space and a crucial concern. To analyze the validity of the claim that AI can be helpful, interaction with GPT-4o is essential to reveal how local knowledge and cultural nuances are handled and responded to. Cultural nuances are understood here as the subtle and unspoken elements of a 'culture' associated with the contextual meanings of certain attitudes or symbols (Olowookere et al., 2021). They comprise proverbs, idiomatic expressions, and clichés (Vishwakarma, 2023) that have to be already known by an AI model for deeper cultural interaction and understanding. In this chapter, we maintain that these nuances are particularities and specificities that could distinguish certain cultures from others.

For example, in the field of translation, a translator is obliged to be conversant with deeper cultural systems, e.g., issues related to death, greeting customs, political concerns, and even dress codes (Vishwakarma, 2023). As it applies here, since we will be comparing some cultural nuances in Moroccan society, mainly endemic in how some Moroccans see or describe themselves, with the assumed Western algorithms of the AI model 'GPT-4o', we realize that there is a slight mismatch between what the model generates and the way we believe, as scholars interested in intercultural communication, cultural nuances might be ideally encoded or reflected. In particular, clothing protocol, as a cultural nuance, can play a pivotal role in conveying both cultural identity and the contexts an individual is representing in Morocco and beyond. While we seek to mitigate the production of, e.g., stereotypes that might reduce Morocco to a single entity, we also wish to explore the possibility that AI

DOI: 10.4324/9781003688853-7

could be trained by ordinary individuals, not designers or engineers, to avoid allegedly 'orientalist' misunderstandings.

In this regard, AI can be useful in disrupting orientalist and exotic images that may represent 'Morocco', 'Africa' and the 'East', as three in one or a blend with no local specificities (Simour, 2020), ignoring how the East and Africa are seen as broad spaces that comprise diverse localities with specific cultures and sets of knowledge (Shakira et al., 2022). Edward Said's (2014) concept of Orientalism – illustrating how Western discourse often constructs the East as exotic, backward, or static in painting and other portrayals – has long been regarded as a cornerstone and a motivator for encouraging skepticism toward matters produced by the West. This tendency to frame non-Western cultures through stereotypes has been described as hegemonic, especially since AI models may continue to represent cultural narratives in the same way, shaped by their Western-based algorithms (Brown et al., 2024). The chapter may seem overambitious in its claim that AI could offer spaces for interaction that are free from the burden of specific ideologies. These spaces – what we will later refer to as lacunae or chatboxes – could contain explored guides that allow users to include their cultural nuances and specificities, helping to avoid, e.g., orientalist associations that overlook local cultures.

5.2 Intercultural communication, AI, and the burden of theory: toward curiosity as an intercultural strategy

Majumdar (2025) describes cultural hegemony as a colonial strategy to control societies politically, culturally, and economically through education, language, and philosophy. He sheds light on traditional rivals, suggesting that the West is perpetually seeking a strategic plan to assert dominance over the East or the Global South. Dervin (2015) argues that one must critically engage with dominant discourses shaped by Western power structures in making sense of interculturality, considering how Western theories and perspectives continue to dominate intercultural communication (R'boul, 2022) exercising the power to decide which knowledge and cultures to include and exclude. Moreover, the perception of the West as the dominant authority in the field of intercultural communication largely stems from the pervasive influence of Western, English-speaking scholars in related research (Dervin et al., 2021). Our central question focuses on whether intercultural communication could still serve as an extension of Western hegemony even after the advent of AI despite the field being widely recognized for promoting tolerance, reducing stereotypes, and encouraging criticality (Neuliep, 2016).

Decoloniality is among these theories that may problematize conversations with AI, when navigating issues of power dynamics. Through our conversation with GPT-4.5, it admitted that having good knowledge of decolonial theories helps challenge Eurocentrism, recognize hidden biases, value marginalized voices, and reach intercultural understanding. We pushed this conversation a little further by asking who would be considered a marginalized voice. The prompt we submitted was as follows: "Who are considered marginalized voices in global discourse?". GPT-4.5 answered by referring to individuals or groups whose perspectives, experiences, and knowledge systems have been historically silenced, undervalued, or excluded from dominant narratives. GPT-4.5 went on to state that these individuals are generally from the Global South – voices from Africa, Latin America, the Middle East, Southeast Asia, and other non-Western localities that are often underrepresented or misrepresented in global discourse, academia, and policy-making. Through our interaction with AI, we discovered that presenting or sharing a culture by locals would be the solution to help one move beyond the never-ending loop of Western-Eastern opposition. It means that sensitive issues that either underrepresent or prioritize certain individuals should be addressed willingly by AI users.

We believe they should be addressed or invoked, as GPT-4.5 responded, within a frame of curiosity, not disrespect. We suggested to GPT-4.5 to consider this as a technique to avoid referencing complex theories and their formal integrity. The prompt submitted was as follows: "Can curiosity-driven cultural sharing work better than relying on academic mediation in resolving misunderstandings?". Shortly before responding to the suggestion, the AI model provided us with a real incident that happened to Syrian refugees after 2015 in a company in Germany. It stated that, at first, there were misunderstandings – e.g., some refugees avoiding eye contact or not shaking hands with female colleagues, which was misread as 'rude'. As a solution, some managers brought in intercultural mediators who explained the cultural norms on both sides and helped them navigate the problem. Our critique prompted the AI model to ask itself why it is always necessary to rely on formalities, formal mediation, and other academic strategies to resolve such misunderstandings. Syrians and Germans could have spoken to each other amiably, asking about (or even criticizing) these sensitive issues purely out of curiosity. Only then could one understand the context in which such behaviors occur – a context of neither harm nor disrespect. Their conversation could be driven by curiosity, surprise, and suspense in the pursuit of intercultural understanding. Surprisingly, GPT-4.5 modeled such a conversation after stating that genuine curiosity should come before formal mediation, calling this principle 'Curiosity-First Interculturality':

Julia (from Sweden): "Hey Omar, I noticed you didn't shake my hand earlier – do you mind if I ask why?".

Omar (from Syria): "Not at all. In my culture, some people avoid handshakes with the opposite gender out of respect or religious reasons. It's nothing personal".

Julia: "Ah, I appreciate you sharing that. Good to know – it helps me understand better".

Our last question was on how AI could apply this principle to its algorithms or its conversation. GPT-4.5 answered:

- AI should not jump straight to *protective*, *formal*, or *overly academic* responses. Instead of saying: "That topic is sensitive; it may reflect colonial power structures…".
- It could first ask: "Are you asking from a cultural curiosity or a personal experience?".
- Rather than automatically avoiding complex topics (like race, religion, or gender), AI can engage gently, like: "That word has a long and painful history for many – are you asking about its origins or how it's used today?".
- AI can demonstrate how to ask difficult questions politely, encouraging users to do the same in their real-life interactions.

One could wonder why GPT-4.5 answered the way it did, as it was possibly 'guided' to answer the question in a way that aligned with our aim. In one of its answers, it wrote that it does not present decolonial theory as a requirement for intercultural communication but rather sees it as a useful lens, especially when deeper issues of power, history, and inequality come into play. Since our conversation with GPT-4.5 was convivial and humorous, we challenged its claim of using decolonial theory as just a lens, not a requirement. We argued that the more we escape the decolonial approach, the closer we get to it. GPT-4.5, in an amused manner ('haha'), restated that the more we escape the decolonial approach, the closer we get to it – just by engaging in real intercultural dialogue. It went on to explain why such a claim might be valid by stating:

- If you're truly open to other cultures,
- If you listen deeply and value non-Western knowledge,
- If you notice power imbalances in the conversation,
- If you question why certain voices are missing…
- *…you're already doing the work that* ***decolonial theory tries to name*** *– even if you never use the word "decolonial".*

This may seem far from revealing or finding alternatives to the intricate integrity of theories that we see drive skepticism toward orientalist applications, yet it can still highlight that very complexity – especially when a local person falls easily victim to subconscious categorization and comparison. This only could revive conflict anew, not reaching any intercultural aims. We could then ask the question: Is AI an extension of Western hegemony, or can it be reclaimed as a truly intercultural space? The next section will take an in-depth look at this.

5.3 AI as mirror and mediator: rethinking bias and culture in intercultural communication

A popular assumption in the media, public, and academia is that AI models are Western inventions and that their underlying applications prioritize Western values. Among these claims, we find one in which Mollema (n.d.) argues that AI embeds social systems that reinforce Western globality. It is referred to as the imposition of Western colonial values on the Global South in the digital sphere, and digital capitalism that blurs local cultural nuances. As one of our foci is examining whether such a claim is valid, and since we see AI as a potentially helpful space for reconciliation that can acknowledge cultural particularities and challenge stereotypes, we chose to investigate this ourselves by closely analyzing AI's responses to see if it addresses some of the facets we know to be part of Moroccan cultures.

We asked GPT-4o to generate an image of a Moroccan teacher in a Moroccan classroom setting by using the prompt: "Can you generate an image of a Moroccan teacher in a Moroccan classroom setting?". What we received was a realistic and somewhat dated image – not in an anime or cartoon-like style – depicting a Moroccan teacher wearing a djellaba, a garment commonly worn in various contexts in Morocco, primarily associated with traditional and religious festivities. The teacher stood in front of four students, with a classroom board behind him showing a map of Morocco. We found that the image reflected some local cultural details without overgeneralizing or reducing Moroccan identity to a single representation. However, since the image depicted a traditional semblance in terms of how the teacher was dressed, we invited GPT to generate a Moroccan teacher wearing a suit. It then provided us with a Moroccan teacher with Moroccan physiognomy, wearing a suit and standing with a board right behind him. We can claim that this was easy because personal photos that are posted or shared online are what AI's performance mostly relies on, as it can depend, above all, on how habitually people converse with it and how often pertinent content is provided. Therefore, it was important for us to think about AI as a virtual space that has no limits in providing what users seek – except when it cannot track the particular information or content they seek. If AI can find what is asked for, it will not hesitate to deliver it.

On social media, some people tend to interact with AI, mainly using it as a space for entertainment, often requesting animated (anime or cartoon-like style) pictures of themselves. Acting similarly, we attempted to generate an animated picture of a Moroccan teacher in a purely Moroccan setting, knowing that we had earlier successfully generated a realistic image of a Moroccan teacher in a local and traditional setting. However, when we later asked for an animated version, the AI program responded with an apology, stating it couldn't generate the requested image. Alternatively, we asked it to produce an animated image of an American teacher in an American setting to see whether it prioritizes Western depictions. This time, we received an animated image of an American teacher wearing a suit, in a classroom with an American flag hanging on the wall, teaching students.

To check whether AI was prioritizing American representations, we immediately asked for an animated image of a Moroccan teacher wearing a suit. The AI model was able to generate it but, this time, the classroom space was not distinguishable from the one in which we saw the American teacher. The settings looked nearly identical. Our aim was for GPT-4o to generate an animated image similar to the earlier one featuring the teacher wearing a djellaba – a garment that has recently been renewed and stylized to reflect Moroccan specificity, not only 'old traditions'. This suggests one key point among others: although media platforms have recently promoted GPT-4o's ability to generate animated images on demand, it may be that GPT-4o's algorithms are still not fully capable of representing cultural nuances and specificities (such as customary clothing) particularly in spaces like classrooms. It feels like the classroom setting and the djellaba-clad teacher are still out of sync.

We then asked GPT-4o to convert the image of djellaba-clad teacher into a cartoon-like image in a Moroccan and modern classroom. It then produced the image as requested, placing it in a modern space it identified as Moroccan. Thus, the Moroccan cultural nuance – which might have been seen as traditional or outdated and not fitting into modern settings through animated pictures – was recontextualized as an element that can adapt to various environments through animated images.

We believe that by interacting with AI and describing cultural specificities, users could contribute to training its algorithms and help include nuanced cultural representations – such as the animated image we generated – within AI's outputs. It is crucial to point out that AI is certainly undergoing continuous development toward unknown strategies that might surpass our expectations. All the ideas we have reached so far may become outdated the moment we finish our conversation. To illustrate this, just two days after writing this section, Moroccan media became filled with AI-generated videos depicting all kinds of Moroccan-specific clothing in various contexts. We would not dare claim that we are responsible for this, and it might have happened before our interaction. To us, AI is complex and must be used wisely: who knows it might tailor or appropriate its responses to just suit the flow or current of the interactors' thoughts.

We could also ask the question: "how about thinking of AI creation as following a pattern of collecting cultural specificities and nuances to shape a comprehensive set of knowledge about the world?". However, this process could remain relative to the interactor – it is up to individuals to delegate and describe their own local realities. The fact that such cultural descriptions are neither banned nor excluded to fit a predetermined agenda in AI's algorithms is particularly significant. Effectively, to maintain a free and equitable digital world, individuals' lived experiences are key to making the world's localities visible, active contributors, and sources of knowledge within AI's chatboxes. This creates a fertile ground for both the West and the East to share and co-construct knowledge, dismantling the idea of dominance or supremacy. Only by recognizing that global knowledge is shaped by individuals' perspectives, each rooted in unique contexts, can we hope for a truly intercultural interaction fed into chatboxes. Only then would we be able to shape a discourse free from the supposed biased tactics that suppress nuanced worldviews, particularly those labeled as exotic or marginal. Epistemic injustices could stem from individuals themselves, who may engage with bias in educating AI's algorithms about what their cultures comprise. AI could be seen as a mirror reflecting what people feed into it; this, in turn, can later be framed or understood as hegemony or bias (see Dervin, 2025). We believe that the process AI is taking represents progress toward 'real' intercultural interaction, as it responds with compliance and does not reject our demands to include or modulate some cultural aspects. What is needed here is encouragement to expand chatboxes and spaces specific to intercultural interaction, not skepticism toward Western applications.

5.4 AI between challenge and escape: GPTs as spaces for free discussions

In Miragoli's (2024) conceptualization regarding the migration of hegemonic discourses from the material to the cyberspace, the need to deeply apply 'hermeneutical lacunae' is an aid, especially in the context of global knowledge and AI. Morgan (2024) pinpoints that hermeneutical lacuna hints at the absence of the interpretive resources that give the possibility to a person to make sense of their experience or to appropriately communicate it to others. This means that it is manifested in the absence of a word or a phrase with which a person could name or contribute an experience. If we were to conceptualize and artificially materialize hermeneutical lacunae, they would take the form of a GPT, an empty space or chatbox designed for including experiences and expanding diverse cultural nuances and specificities.

Our next interaction with GPT-4o was based on this principle of hermeneutical lacunae, through which we endeavored to examine how GPT-4o would respond to the inclusion of cultural specificities in its varied GPTs. While trying to interact with GPT-4o, we discovered that these GPTs are AI chatbots or models put in GPT-4o, serving as options for one to 'swim' within their area of focus. Among these GPTs of different domains and areas, we found some specialized in education, writing, and research, while others were related to productivity and programming. After discovering that each GPT contained branches of a specific domain, we looked into the one specialized in lifestyle. It was completely devoid of anything related to culture and its diverse lifestyles or nuances.

We asked GPT-4o whether it could create a model designed to learn from and promote the lifestyles and cultures of specific localities worldwide. The prompt was as follows: "Can you create or propose a GPT that is designed to learn from and promote the lifestyles and cultures of specific localities around the world?". While it offered theoretical frameworks, conceptual designs, and suggestions, it proposed that the actual implementation of a GPT for including cultures would need to be carried out by a team of specialists and designers who can integrate the necessary data sources, algorithms, and ethical safeguards. This can be understood as a challenge, but only in a way that advocates for complex theoretical integrity and demands. We were not surprised by GPT-4o's answer that the addition of a space or GPT involves collaboration with AI designers, cultural experts or theorists, and engineers. This theorist-based conclusion makes us feel that we are guided to no other end than the decolonial approach again, perhaps not allowing freedom for curious interaction. Here, as we stated in the above sections, the interaction of normal or non-academic people within the invocation of theories could feel a bit complicated, raising fears of having to align with theoretical requirements. Also, one could argue that non-academic individuals, through their everyday interactions and contributions, may serve as important agents in shaping intercultural realities within AI models, especially in increasingly digital and globally connected contexts.

GPT might be prompted to add a space itself since its data are trained to evolve and adapt to new ways of reasoning (Arcas, 2025), especially when it comes to culture. In its answer, GPT-4o called the GPT space we asked for a 'PolylogueGPT', which it referred to as a space containing diverse perspectives and cultures. This proposed system is driven by the aim of creating an interculturally aware GPT that contextualizes cultural information or nuances, detects and adjusts bias, and encourages intercultural dialogue through dynamic learning and interactivity. This space would rely on data sources evolved from diverse localities, including ethnographic research, historical texts, and global media, while integrating feedback and collaborating with cultural experts. Key principles would include interactive modes and ethical considerations, which would help the GPT with bias detection, sensitivity testing, and indigenous knowledge protection. Within a decolonial framework, GPT-4o proposed that the focus would be chiefly on transparency and inclusive feedback loops. It defined 'inclusive feedback loops' as a strategy or processes that interactively collect input, reactions, and specific concepts from a wide and diverse range of input to ameliorate the system continuously toward intercultural understanding. Ultimately, the goal would be to build an accessible, scalable AI tool for use in education, media, and global business. We postulate that a space or GPT which could be on offer without academic requirements would be easy for individuals to include and share their cultures freely, without subconscious chains driving them away, fearing not to meet the requirements on display.

Additionally, there appears to be a semiotic explanation for this since the theory-based requirements offered in chatboxes might be a symbolic aspect activating one's mind map (Hall, 1997). This is to remind their hegemonic-decolonial theories, igniting desires to challenge and doubt the chatbox of its supposedly inherent Western bias. These requirements could also represent complexities to delay any intercultural communication in AI's chatboxes. Our last question directed to GPT was about the possibility of designing a space by itself without the intervention of theorists, designers, or any inclusion of theoretical requirements, just by being prompted by local individuals. The prompt was as follows: "Can you design or help create a GPT that is entirely based on input from local individuals, without relying on academic theorists or formal designers?". It answered that, in principle, it is possible to design a specialized GPT, or a 'PolylogueGPT', that focuses on cultural nuances and helps collect what people think and experience across different localities. The surprise was that GPT proposed and provided a model to co-design a PolylogueGPT with local individuals, illustrating the model as follows:

1 Start with listening

    - Ask: "What do you want this space to do for you?"
    - Collect stories, emotions, silences – not just needs but tones and fears
    - Let their language shape the system – not translated but held as it is

2 Design pillars

    - Curiosity-led: GPT asks, never assumes
    - Non-extractive: users decide what stays, what goes
    - Fragment-friendly: not everything needs to be whole or explained
    - Context-aware: GPT adapts tone to cultural rhythms (formality, silence, indirectness)

3 Interaction model

    - Users can:
        - Share thoughts (voice, text, story)
        - Choose to stay anonymous or present
        - Pause, revise, or retract anything
        - GPT responds like a curious listener, not a teacher or analyst:
        - "Would you like to expand on that?"
        - "What does this mean in your world?"

4 Cultural memory layer

    - With consent, stories can form part of a living memory archive
    - Local people name and tag their own experiences, not external categories

5 Local stewardship

    - Community selects guardians or stewards, not moderators
    - Their role: care, not control – ensuring dignity, not enforcing rules.

GPT even asked if we would like a prototype dialogue or an interface concept to see how this model might feel in action. It then created this dialogue:

User:	In Morocco, I wear a djellaba almost every day – not just for Fridays or weddings.
PolylogueGPT:	That's interesting. What does the djellaba mean to you in your everyday life?
User:	It feels like continuity – like I'm part of something older, even when I'm just walking to the café.
PolylogueGPT:	I like that. What would you want someone outside Morocco to understand about the djellaba?
User:	That it's not just for religious or traditional moments. In the countryside, people wear it daily – for work, markets, and visits. It brings a kind of quiet respect, and it fits anywhere.
PolylogueGPT:	It sounds like it carries dignity and flexibility.
User:	Yes – and it's useful too. It protects from heat and cold. It's a kind of clothing that understands the weather before you do.

References

Arcas, B. a. Y. (2025, April 11). *AI is evolving — and changing our understanding of intelligence*. NOEMA. https://www.noemamag.com/ai-is-evolving-and-changing-our-understanding-of-intelligence/

Brown, V., Larasati, R., Third, A., & Farrell, T. (2024). A qualitative study on cultural hegemony and the impacts of AI. *Proceedings of the AAAI/ACM Conference on AI, Ethics, and Society*, *7*, 226–238. https://doi.org/10.1609/aies.v7i1.31632

Dervin, F. (2015). *Interculturality in education: A theoretical and methodological toolbox*. Springer.

Dervin, F. (2025). *AI for critical interculturality*. Routledge.

Dervin, F., Sude, Yuan, M., & Chen, N. (2021). *Interculturality between East and West: Unthink, dialogue, rethink*. Springer Nature.

Hall, S. (1997). *Representation: Cultural representations and signifying practices*. SAGE.

Kay, J., Kasirzadeh, A., & Mohamed, S. (2024). Epistemic injustice in generative ai. *Proceedings of the AAAI/ACM Conference on AI, Ethics, and Society*, *7*, 684–697. https://doi.org/10.1609/aies.v7i1.31671

Majumdar, S. (2025). Cultural hegemony: Colonial obligation, Swadeshi resistance and globalization in India from the British to the contemporary era. *International Journal for Multidisciplinary Research*, *7*(1). https://doi.org/10.36948/ijfmr.2025.v07i01.35885

Miragoli, M. (2024). Conformism, ignorance & injustice: AI as a tool of epistemic oppression. *Episteme*, 1–19. https://doi.org/10.1017/epi.2024.11

Mollema, W. J. T. (n.d.). Decolonial AI as disenclosure. *Open Journal of Social Sciences*, *12*(02), 574–603. https://doi.org/10.4236/jss.2024.122032

Morgan, R. (2024). Hermeneutical disarmament. *The Philosophical Quarterly*. https://doi.org/10.1093/pq/pqae046

Neuliep, J. W. (2016). *Intercultural communication: A contextual approach*. SAGE Publications.

Olowookere, E. I., Agoha, B. C., Omonijo, D. O., Odukoya, J. A., & Elegbeleye, A. O. (2021). Cultural nuances in work attitudes and behaviors: Towards a model of African work culture. *Academic Journal of Interdisciplinary Studies*, *10*(2), 259. https://doi.org/10.36941/ajis-2021-0056

R'boul, H. (2022). Postcolonial interventions in intercultural communication knowledge: Meta-intercultural ontologies, decolonial knowledges and epistemological polylogue. *Journal of International and Intercultural Communication*, *15*(1), 75–93. https://doi.org/10.1080/17513057.2020.1829676

Said, E. W. (2014). *Orientalism*. Vintage.

Shakira, F. D., Najimy, K., Mitchell, G., Hayek, S., & Abraham, S. (2022, October 28). Facts about Arabs and the Arab World. *ADC - Truly Arab, Fully American*. https://adc.org/facts-about-arabs-and-the-arab-world/#:~:text=Iran%20and%20Turkey%20are%20not%20Arab%20countries%20and,and%20others.%20There%20are%20over%20300%20million%20Arabs.

Simour, L. (2020). Gendered eyewitness in narration: Imagining Morocco in British women travel-inspired narratives in late nineteenth century. *Anglo Saxónica/Anglo SaxóNica*, *17*(1). https://doi.org/10.5334/as.22

Vishwakarma, V. K. (2023). Translating cultural nuances: Challenges and strategies. *Zenodo (CERN European Organization for Nuclear Research)*.

Wisner, W. (2023, May 26). *Cultural awareness—How to be more culturally aware & improve your relationships*. Verywell Mind. https://www.verywellmind.com/cultural-awareness-importance-how-to-develop-it-7500316

6 In search of justifiable AI governance for Africa

Isaiah A. Negedu and Oluwaseun T. Babatuyi

6.1 Introduction

The rapid development of science and technology comes with many promises, making the lives of humans more liveable. They contribute a great deal to what makes the world a 'global village'. At the same time, their applications across various environments tend to generate some concerns that revolve around contextual issues, which are hinged on the fact that humans belong to different cultures and societies, and sometimes, values may also differ. While most parts of the Global North and some parts of the Global South appear to benefit from their rapid development, in most parts of Africa, the development of science and technology has not been characterised by the same pace (Kahn, 2022, p. 345). Within the context of our research, digital technologies are considered especially in relation to the Fourth Industrial Revolution (4IR). Every revolution (from the first to the fourth) has its inventors and/or major proponents from nations that are considered either developed and/or industrialised. It is not out of place for the countries that are hosts to any form of technology to be the first and probably major beneficiaries of any new technology, before exporting it to other parts of the world.

The Silicon Valley in the USA is particularly known for its consistent advancement in technology as it is home to multiple notable start-ups and tech firms, including Facebook, Apple and Google. Also, South Korea and Taiwan are not left out as they are well advanced in the development of some digital infrastructure, such as semiconductors and electronics. The problem with such development emanates from the fact that other countries are not swiftly involved, mostly because, beyond providing goods and services for humanity, people involved in the business of digital technologies rely on the neoliberal principle of the free market with capitalist motives (Hendrix, 2025; Hoffman, 2023; Lu, 2020; Sadowski, 2016). However, this version of neoliberalism is tilted towards capitalist principles of individual ownership and control. It is at this juncture and with this mindset that Africa could become a victim in ideological and economic terms, much more than being a major beneficiary of digital technologies. In order to ensure that every country in the world is

DOI: 10.4324/9781003688853-8

carried along on the path to digital technologies, we will examine the concept of justice and see how it could operate in relation to AI. In so doing, we also interrogate the place of Africa (sub-Saharan and North Africa) in the 4IR and make a case for interculturally competent experts to be drafted in the development of algorithms for digital technologies.

6.2 Interrogating the concept of justice

To appreciate the justifiability of AI in Africa, justice as an important moral concept needs to be interrogated. Doing this requires a consideration of both Western and African notions of justice. This is not only because justice has practical applications to AI Governance but also because it may be regarded as a dominant virtue with a foundational impact on all other moral discourses. More importantly, there can be no basis for AI governance without a nuanced conception of justice that eliminates unfair treatments. As a result of its multiple uses, justice is regarded as somewhat controversial (Ojimba, 2018). Justice has to do with "right or regulation" emanating from the Latin etymology "jus". In a slightly similar vein, the Yoruba African conception of justice originates from the word "títọ́" which simply means "rightness or appropriateness" of human conduct, including actions, choices and decisions. Consequently, justice implies acts that are considered appropriate, right or done in accordance with regulation. Away from this conception of justice, we thus interrogate the concept from the perspectives of some prominent scholars with the intent of establishing an apposite foundation for its applicability to AI Governance.

To start with, justice was conceived as the mechanism for functionality and harmony within the individual and society by the Ancient Greek philosopher Plato (427–347 B.C.E.). In his notable work, *The Republic*, he considered justice in the individual as possessing three properties, namely, wisdom, temperance and courage, which respectively imply justice of the mind, the senses and the heart (Plato, 2007). By extension, justice in society indicates right living and adherence to the regulations of the State. This notion of justice recognises classes in a given society and the need for different parts to function with the consciousness of their limits and respect for individual boundaries. While Plato's theory helps in providing an ideal concept of justice and sheds light on how justice operates in an individual and the State, it fails to define justice in clear terms and cannot establish how individuals and the State can act justly.

Thomas Aquinas (Italy, 1224–1274; see Aquinas, 1947, p. 11, 54, a.3), among other medieval scholars, posits that justice is "the firm and constant will to give to each one his due". In other words, it is a moral virtue where fairness is ensured while interacting with others. Justice was regarded as the law of God or as a part of the natural law whereby everyone is basically considered to be equal and should be treated equally. When two persons have acted in a particular way, it would only amount to injustice if the consequences are not the same. The virtue of justice demands that human actions are always in alliance with the law of nature. This notion from Aquinas helps to understand justice as a fundamental entitlement of everyone and that no one deserves to be treated unjustly. However, it does not take into consideration the fact that nature itself does not present things equally. For instance, there are different creatures within the universe demonstrating varying degrees of capacities and characteristics. Among human beings, we often talk of individual differences and dimensions of strength and weakness. Traveling from one part of the globe to another, one sees variations in topography and distribution of natural resources. The ideas of nature and natural law do not automatically imply fairness and equitable distribution or allocation of things.

The modern conception of justice is found in two major dimensions, which are justice as duty-based and justice as utility-based. From the perspective of Immanuel Kant (Germany, 1724–1804), justice is conceived as a moral obligation that is absolutely necessary and binding on all, irrespective of the accompanying consequences. Kant (1994), through his categorical imperative, presents justice and formulates it on three major propositions, namely: (a) justice or a just act must be universalisable; (b) justice or a just act must consider the intrinsic or inherent values of things – in other words, it must not treat anyone or anything as a means to an end but as an end in themselves; (c) justice or a just act must consider humans as rational and autonomous moral beings. Thus, according to Kant, commitment to moral duties and respect for individual rights, freedom and autonomy are the fundamentals of justice. The notion of justice in Kant's perspective is highly commendable, as no condition is expected to be met before acting in a just way. Yet, the view lacks a comprehensive account of the motivation for acting justly because the consideration of intrinsic values can, in some cases, be insufficient. The current age of AI, for instance, has shown that practical impact and utility values cannot be ignored in the determination of what counts as justice or otherwise.

In another vein, justice has been described by Jeremy Bentham (England, 1748–1832) and John Stuart Mill (England, 1806–1873) as something that is utility-based because acting justly simply implies fulfilling some utilitarian conditions. Justice does not necessarily require respect for autonomy and some intrinsic values. Put differently, an act is just, according to this perspective, if and only if it produces the greatest happiness for the greatest number of people. Mill's (1863) proposition for justice is in accordance with "proportion as they tend to promote happiness", and by happiness, he refers to "intended pleasure and the absence of pain" (pp. 9–10). Thus, justice is determined by the consequences produced by an act, especially such that the outcome results in great pleasure or happiness rather than pain. The relevance of this utility-based conception of justice cannot be overemphasised, as it agrees with most basic common-sense explanations for acting right or justly. Nevertheless, justice from a utilitarian understanding is not all-encompassing as it fails to accommodate everyone and treat all with fairness. The minority are possibly going to suffer some forms of oppression, marginalisation and injustice, if such a theory should be taken seriously.

So far, we have examined some perspectives on justice which exemplify various notions of moral justice within Western thought. We have also demonstrated how these notions of justice are troubled by an array of unfeasible and controversial standpoints. While the logical construction of these notions of justice is appreciated, the emotional colouration with which they are presented as impeccably sufficient theories represents a potential cause for concern. There ought to be something emanating from our shared humanity that prioritises fair and equal treatment of others. The moral virtue of justice should therefore be more encompassing in a way that human existential realities are accommodated, especially in an age where the existence of intelligent machines is somewhat threatening human existence, through attacks, abuse and manipulations by cyber criminals and other human beings. We shall now turn to some African perspectives for further interrogation of the notion of justice. Within the African thought systems, as observable in some parts of the continent, justice takes a slight departure from the Western worldview.

Justice, like other primary principles of moral values such as freedom, human dignity and truth, is considered in Africa as a universal principle that is fundamental to law and morality (Azenabor, 2022, p. 68). Unlike the Western conception, the African thought system understands justice as a moral principle that enhances communal cohesion, while the individual welfare is equally promoted. Two prominent concepts can be used to further describe justice in African thought systems: Ubuntu and Omoluabi.

Ubuntu captures the idea of justice based on its notion of human interconnectedness, through which it prioritises not only the direct impacts of an individual's action on the overall well-being of others but also promotes commitments to being good to one another. Lutz (2024), for instance, sees Ubuntu and justice as the same, as they constitute a central component of African traditional thought relating to morality, politics and society. Thus, Ubuntu is translatable to humanity, humanness or humaneness (Lutz, 2024, p. 21; see Chapter 7 of this volume). Justice, from this understanding, embraces the centrality of the human face in our actions and promotes commitment to shared responsibility for the well-being of others. Any action that fails to consider humanity first or being human or humane in the scheme of things will be regarded as unjust. Also, when an action is not done with the underlying motivation of enhancing the welfare of others and taking responsibility for others, it is considered unjust.

Similarly, Omoluabi is a Yoruba moral concept from Nigeria that describes a person who acts justly or virtuously. Consequently, to be an Omoluabi is to be a just person or a person who is committed to justice. By its equivalency to justice, it is aptly considered as a value system that allows for preferences, choices and moderations with high regard for honour and integrity (Azenabor, 2022, pp. 65–66). This conception of justice promotes compassion, cooperation and camaraderie in human society such that every individual with this ideal mindset lives with the consciousness of responsibility and accountability to others.

Interrogating justice from the foregoing accentuates certain virtues such as truth, transparency, inclusiveness and balance among others in moral conduct. The conceptualisations of justice from the African notions of Ubuntu and Omoluabi provide a more assuring hope, especially in the face of challenges posed by the sophistication and complications that come with AI inventions. The complex structure of AI developments can come along with certain sentiments built into them by their developers, thereby resulting in unfair treatment of human beings, violation of human rights or deliberate marginalisation of certain groups of people. For instance, studies have shown that facial recognition software has higher error rates for people of colour. Particularly, most algorithms seem to substantially fail in correctly identifying Black women more than members of any other demography (Findley, 2020, para 1). This is where the understanding of justice from an African perspective becomes handy. Its principle of interconnectedness could help ensure humane and fair treatment and consideration of people irrespective of their socio-cultural background. In the same manner, it could help remove possible bias in the data and AI algorithms for non-discriminatory presentation of information. Similarly, through its commitment to truth and transparency, there would be no hidden or inaccessible clauses in the decision-making process of AI systems.

Therefore, the need for a well-structured approach to the regulation and maintenance of AI cannot be overemphasised if accountability and responsibility are not compromised. There is a need for a well-structured approach to the regulation and maintenance of AI, such that it guarantees accountability and responsibility. The individualistic and humanistic conceptions of justice from the Western worldviews may be susceptible to loss of core human values due to emphasis on autonomy, equality, freedom or egalitarianism, among others. For instance, when focus is only on individual well-being, there could be a detraction from collective responsibilities and social justice. Also, when individual quests for self-actualisation are enabled, communal and economic imperatives are at stake (Leyva, 2025, para. 10). However, an honest consideration of justice from the African notion of interconnectedness could provide the desired raw material for a well-balanced and well-regulated moral life in the 4IR age. It could also help in confronting varieties of developmental, existential and moral concerns arising from the growing advancement of AI. Given the understanding that concerted efforts are being deployed to ensure AI governance in the world, the understanding of justice in African perspectives would certainly shape a form of AI governance to be embraced in Africa.

6.3 Some principles for AI governance

Any growth, if not maintained or regulated, may be hazardous both to itself and the human environment. This also applies to the continuous advancement being recorded in digital technologies with the help of AI. Ensuring that AI is developed and deployed sustainably and profitably has become a genuine concern for some (non)governmental agencies, ethicists and policymakers. Being a human invention, its vulnerability to certain sentiments and infringements of people's rights are potential dangers that cannot be ruled out. McNeilly (2023) has shown that people who belong to any underrepresented group, for instance, can be denied the right to employment if historical recruitment records reveal a preference for candidates from a particular background. This is because an AI model will learn to favour candidates from the historically preferred background. Given the increasing technological advancement, the term AI governance has become a necessary part of our vocabularies. Mucci (2024) captures AI governance as the guardrails, processes and standards through which the safety and morality of AI tools are guaranteed. This includes the provision of frameworks that watch over the research, development and application of AI such that fairness, respect and safety for human rights are ensured. It is not enough to have policies and structures in place to govern the making and the use of AI; it must be accompanied by stringent monitoring mechanisms that address potential dangers.

Given the sophisticated nature of AI, regulatory oversight might involve evaluation, monitoring and updating of data and machine learning algorithms. AI governance can thus ensure that the intelligent display of digital technologies is not at variance with societal norms and moral expectations. To ensure accountability and responsibility in the use of AI, different programmes, policies and practices are being adopted by organisations and government agencies as forms of AI governance approaches. Cases and contexts of AI governance identified by Mucci (2024) include the following: (a) the European Union's General Data Protection Regulation (GDPR), which ensures personal data and privacy are protected; (b) The Organisation for Economic Co-operation and Development (OECD), which emphasises transparency, fairness and accountability in AI systems as responsible stewardship of trustworthy AI; and (c) Corporate AI Ethics Boards (CAIEB), which are formed by different organisations to ensure compliance and alignment of AI policies with societal values and ethical standards.

What are the principles of AI Governance? Every policy or programme that intends to regulate human activities, including inventions such as digital technologies, ought to be based on sound philosophy (for instance, such that can preserve human dignity and environmental safety), which will serve as the springboard for compliance. These philosophies, in the case of AI governance, are regarded as principles that are basic to the ethical and responsible deployment of AI. *First,* such principles are considered ethical because they ensure that the morality of AI systems is not compromised from invention to implementation. By this, all kinds of injustice against people (e.g., invasion of privacy and disregard for human dignity) can be prevented. *Second,* such principles are adjudged to be responsible insofar they ensure sentiments, secrecy and marginalisation (which are potential harmful consequences) are reduced if not expunged from the functionality of AI systems (Batool et al., 2025, para. 1). Essentially, trust, transparency, accountability, empathy, explainability, safety, security, fairness, inclusiveness, reproducibility, robustness, bias-control and data governance are identified (among others) as fundamental principles of AI governance. The list of these principles can be summed up through the principles of ethics and responsibility, where trust and respect for moral boundaries can be guaranteed. Nevertheless, we adopt and make a cursory mention of five categories of principles for AI governance as submitted by the European Insurance and Occupational Pensions Authority's Consultative Expert Group on Digital Ethics in Insurance (EIOPA, 2021). This choice is based on the support provided for overall AI governance as well as the respect for human dignity.

The first principle is fairness and non-discrimination, which requires that injustice and sentiments be avoided as much as possible in AI development and deployment of AI algorithms as well as applications. The second principle is transparency and explainability, which are closely connected to the first, the grounding rules for the ethics of trustworthiness and accountability in the use and governance of AI. The third principle is data governance and record keeping, which enhances other issues like data quality, integrity and respect for privacy. The fourth principle is robustness and performance, which handles technical and ethical implications of not causing harm. The last principle is human oversight, which ensures that potential dangers to human existence and the environment are prevented. When these principles are integrated into AI governance, ethical and responsible functionality of AI could be achieved. At this point, is it not worthwhile to examine Africa's place in the entire framework of AI governance?

6.4 Where is Africa in the global AI governance?

Based on African perspectives, we refer to governance as the set of frameworks, policies and regulations that are constantly being developed in African nations to ensure the ethical and responsible use of AI technologies. Africa has its unique challenges because the continent is mainly a consumer rather than a producer of AI technologies. This has also widened the digital divide, thereby leading to some form of digital colonialism, which is the extraction of data from individuals with or without their explicit consent for profit (Coleman, 2019, pp. 422–423). It is on this note that we interrogate Africa's place in the governance of digital technologies. This is important to mitigate potential harm and promote equitable access to digital technologies in the 4IR. With a population of over one billion, Africa has been described as a continent that is neither fully in the Global North nor South, but at the centre. The continent's economic growth and rising young population are replete with some hope (Mpemba & Munyati, 2023).

At the same time, being at the centre is fragile for the continent and could be a meeting point where the traditional Global North and South meet to exploit its potential if there is a lack of preparedness on the part of African people. It is therefore not enough to be a consumer of digital technologies without localising the production system to fully harness the benefits of technology. Although many African countries such as Morocco, Tunisia, South Africa and Nigeria (Teleanu & Kurbalija, 2022) have produced strategies for AI governance, and some have also developed legislations to regulate the digital space, there is little control the continent has on the process of invention since tech firms will most likely be regulated largely by digital laws in their different countries of domicile. If Africa is only a recipient and not a valuable contributor to the invention of digital technology, it will lead to the invasion of different rights of the African people, one of which would be privacy concerns.

One of the problems that could arise out of low indigenous contributions is the lack of domestication of AI policies that could lead to breaches of individual privacy and national security. Without indigenous algorithm experts from the African continent to mediate, Africa would end up mortgaging a very important aspect of their existence to external agents who would then monitor and regulate information that should be shared. Because large amounts of personal information put together can be used to identify potential threats, track individuals or even manipulate populations, these could represent serious risks to a country's stability and security, especially when sensitive information about critical infrastructure, military personnel or government officials is involved. A nation whose security is under threat would also be subjected to a deterioration of its national sovereignty. No nation can afford to outsource its security.

The right to privacy is protected by several international documents, including Article 12 of the Universal Declaration of Human Rights (UDHR), Article 17 of the International Covenant on Civil and Political Rights (ICCPR) and Article 10 of the African Charter on the Rights and Welfare of the Child (ACRWC). However, big tech companies have taken advantage of technology to invade the digital space of individuals without their consent. Some notable companies have been implicated in such a privacy breach (Beloume, 2023), which questions our earlier claim of the role of technology for exploitation in the guise of making Africa more 'modern'. This could also be seen through the sale of personal information of people by tech companies to data brokers who use this data to conduct some predictive advertising based on the needs of people. In all this, little has been achieved in the area of fairness in AI governance.

The activities of tech giants, therefore, can lead to data being primarily collected for exploitative ends and not for a people-centred agenda. Google and Facebook enable advertising on the private conversations of their users, making it clear that they will keep exploiting the situation since they make profits from the adverts. Thus, tech firms have become enablers of surveillance capitalism (Zuboff, 2019, p. 47). There are also recorded cases of people's data being harvested and sold online by hackers (Tidy, 2021). Different countries in Africa have their own sets of moral standards, and the capitalists' use of digital technologies is a deviation from the African-centred concept of the human person as a relational entity. The reductionist agenda of people to numeric data stands in opposition to the concept of personhood in Africa, as can also be found in some other parts of the world. Humans are persons and not numbers. To this end, and to the extent that people are reduced to numbers, they are also objectified. When brought together in a community of relationships, each individual is a subject and should be accorded some dignity. According to Birhane (2020):

> The reduction of complex social problems to a matter that can be "solved" by technology also treats people as passive objects for manipulation. Humans, however, far from being passive objects, are active meaning seekers embedded in dynamic social, cultural, and historical backgrounds.
>
> (p. 397)

By acknowledging the challenges and limitations and by employing strategies and technical approaches that prioritise contextual sensitivity and value alignment, AI systems could effectively operate in multicultural environments with diverse ethical values.

Actors in different inventions have always deviated from the original intentions of inventors to the detriment of humans. That was the case with Alfred Binet (Carr, 2024), Tim Berners-Lee (Gunaratna, 2017) and J. Robert Oppenheimer (Little, 2023), who have been credited with different inventions. At various times, they all expressed concerns about the manipulation or misuse of their inventions for profitable ends without ethical considerations (Zhu et al., 2024). Like these inventors, the hope is that AI could become a force for good. Geoffrey Hinton, who is seen as the godfather of AI, is also worried about what it could become (Goodyear, 2023; Schulze, 2019). The anxiety of inventors from one generation to another stems from the fact that technology is driven by capitalist motives that are most likely to prioritise profits over human well-being. This then provides a clue into the progression of AI in the future. Considering how strong nations tend to lead the business of driving AI inventions, and by implication developing policies, where does that leave economically weaker countries, especially in Africa?

The necessity of this reflection stems from the fact that it is difficult to convince a country to tone down on a 'superiorist' agenda (Al Mutawa, 2009; Hauge, 2024). Superiorist thinking places itself above the other and makes itself a benchmark for the other. There is an attempt to pretentiously objectify some other nations in the process of testing the workability of a new technology. It means that there is a greater task on the part of countries that have always played the role of mere recipients of new inventions. One of the ways to cope in the midst of superiorism is for different nations to come up with workable AI policy frameworks that preserve the sovereignty of each country, while at the same time not infringing on the sovereignty of others. This would also involve coping mechanisms, for example, through new alliances that respect the national sovereignty of others, while at the same time focusing on alternative economic policies that would not have adverse effects as a result of new alliances.

Since tech firms are driven by capitalist motives of profit over human welfare, it is not unusual for them to also make provisions for propaganda research in their budgets. This has always been the trajectory, generally of some firms with products that are most likely to have adverse effects. An example of this can be seen in the tobacco industry, where industrialists sponsored propaganda to justify that their product is not dangerous to health (Rabin-Havt & Media Matters for America, 2016). The implication is that these firms dictate morality. Since research is largely propelled by the availability of grants, firms that hope for the greatest profits will also invest in the academic space in the guise of funding research. The danger in such investments is that scholars whose duty it is to maintain some level of integrity in research will be rendered vulnerable to produce determined results in their research by any means necessary.

This should also serve as a lesson for the African continent, where in some countries, there is sluggishness in providing adequate budgets for research (Ger et al., 2024). There is a need to have not just an ethics lab in different regions of the African continent but an independent department of ethics with its own budget in each African country and also funded partly by the private sector. This ethics department should not be driven by profits, and it should be managed by people who have distinguished themselves in scholarship and in character. The purpose of nominating individuals with character is due to the nature of the responsibility, which is ethics-driven. This can best be achieved by ascertaining that the election process, which brings leaders to power, is also not fraught with anomalies. Although it is expected that profits should not be the driving force, this could also help the government in saving funds from its recommendations. This can happen, for instance, if there is credible evidence that noncompliance or involvement in certain activities would be hazardous to society. We tend towards this public-private partnership arrangement because a sensitive unit left fully in the hands of the government has the capacity of being 'bastardised' and, if left in the hands of the private sector, would incur some vested interests.

6.5 The making of interculturally competent experts

To capture the meaning of intercultural competence, it is essential to differentiate between the 'multicultural' and the 'intercultural'. While the former could refer to the existence of several 'cultures' living together, often without significant interaction, the latter could emphasise active communication and interaction between people from different backgrounds (Liu, 2024). Essentially, multiculturalism describes a diverse population belonging to different cultures and each culture in return maintaining its distinctiveness, while contributing to the overall good of the society. One implication of living in a multicultural society is that it can promote coexistence, yet at the same time, different communities may engage less with each other, potentially leading to the formation of parallel societies.

Interculturality (this is one definition among many, see introduction to this volume) speaks to the process of engaging with diversity through dialogue and understanding (United Nations Educational, Scientific and Cultural Organization, 2024). Kastoryano (2018) summarises the differences between the multicultural and the intercultural as follows: proponents of interculturality state that it is not enough for people to live together in a community, they should interact to harness and enjoy the benefits of communion. To speak of interculturality necessarily means the presence of the multicultural, and this can exist in any society where one can find multiple cultures. When relationships transcend individual levels, they sometimes have a political undertone because of the power dynamics which play out between different cultures. What enables such dynamics is the fact that population is sometimes a factor in determining the culture that would be classified along minority and majority lines. Also, relationships can be exploited to serve the aim of cultures that are dominant based on their economic-political influence. Irrespective of the nature of relations mong cultures, interculturality is said to prioritise promoting cultural diversity by systematically transforming asymmetrical relations through development of redemptive channels of participation in the society (Dietz, 2018, p. 3). When people interact, a sense of globalisation could be developed and universal applications of policies rendered more effective.

In the absence of interculturally competent algorithm experts, AI systems can face significant challenges when operating in either intercultural or multicultural environments where ethical values differ. There is a need for human agents who are knowledgeable about intercultural relations to also bring their expertise to bear in AI governance. What is considered legal in the USA may be considered illegal in Nigeria. A good example is the lesbian, gay, bisexual, transgender, and queer (LGBTQ+) laws in both the USA and Nigeria, where it is legal in the former and illegal in the latter. It means that there would be a need for a different AI system that would be wired to work in both societies. A careful study of Sarwari et al. (2024) shows that value alignment is thus a major barrier to the effective use of AI in the world; we live in societies with multiple identities, and people can have different and similar perspectives. The moralities of different societies are also tied to their indigenous cultures.

If that is the case, then algorithm experts have not shown enough willingness to consider every society with its different cultures towards maintaining some fairness in digital technologies. Since AI systems can perpetuate biases

(Ghaffary, 2019), depending on the algorithm that humans feed into them, if trained on biased data or designed with narrow perspectives, it is usually the dominant groups that benefit from such injustices. Examples are Compute North Nations that are host to major digital data and are at the centre in influencing digital policies that regulate global digital space, such as the USA and China (Lehdonvirta et al., 2024). Although different contexts can be complex and nuanced, making it difficult for AI systems to fully understand and adapt to local ethical values, data policies and technology laws of a given country play a greater role in the application of laws. The challenge here will be how to maintain a value-neutral system that is intentional about the existence of the world as a 'true' global village.

A value-neutral system makes it possible to maintain an unbiased stance on any issues. It means, in the first place, a study of the conditions necessary for a subject and how it is applied in each society. Then, the next step would be a search for a meeting point based on the varying applications in each society. When we refer to AI systems, we also know that on their own, they cannot regulate themselves. By this, we mean that there is always a need for algorithm experts to also ensure that certain prompts are carried out and/or wired into the system for AI to work effectively. It is for this reason that our emphasis is on algorithm experts with some level of intercultural competence, who also have the disposition to ensure that there is a prompt that can auto-regulate the system to attend to societal specificities. By this, we mean that people from different countries and cultures should be open to learn the peculiarities of other cultures. The next question would probably be: "How could this be made possible?". We believe that if we are going to think of Artificial General Intelligence (AGI), which is a hypothetical position where machines can do all that humans can do (which would lead to a posthumanist world), then humans should be open to every possible instance that would make such a world achievable. We also do not believe the system can fail as if it regulates itself. Systems are being regulated by human experts, so their failure should also mean the failure of human agents (and in this case: experts).

The next key question is: "whose responsibility is it to ensure cognitive and social justice and fairness in the development of AI?". When people develop problem-solving models, people tend, first, to look at the challenges in their environments and conceptualise solutions that fit specific contexts. Solutions can be universalisable, but that is usually done with the modifications of those solutions in a new recipient environment that was not originally in the mind of the problem solvers. It is the knowledge of a particular environment that strongly determines an appropriate model that would work for such an environment. Most solutions that have a global outlook are first of all *local*, some with the capacity for universalisability, while others tend to be absolutistic. The evolution of social media networks is originally tied to the provision of local solutions in the USA and has evolved into different brands responsible for meeting global needs (Maryville University, 2020).

As an ideology, there are also global feminist movements, which first began as responses to discrimination against women in American society. In 1848, the Women's Rights Convention was held in America with a call for reforms that laid the path to equality globally. Although prior to 1848, there was the French Revolution in 1789 that triggered French women to advocate for their rights (Lindemann, 2023; National Women's History Museum, 2021). The difference between a solution that is universal and one that is absolute is that the former does not desire to enter a territory with the intention of compelling a people to accept a solution without review. The latter imposes a solution on people, denying them the possibility to think and operate in their own terms. Neoliberal engagements have such a tendency, and these are all features a society should pay attention to in relation to AI fairness.

It would be a misnomer for a recipient society to wait for inventors to modify their inventions to suit the recipient environment. A society knows best what should work for them, and if they are intentional about the values that they want to incorporate in any invention before it is utilised in their environments, then it is their task to begin to create their own 'silicon valleys' to partner with developed societies for their own local programmes. The experiences of the Chinese and Japanese have taught nations in the Global South that it is possible to domesticate AI. China uses virtual reality to preserve compromised cultural artefacts. Japan, on the other hand, is investing in digitising the production process of handicrafts (Yang et al., 2024, p. 5).

Chonka et al. (2023) and Salami (2024, p. 3) have also identified a usually ignored issue that revolves around algorithm autocomplete, which suggests the complete characters of a word once an individual starts typing, and how this could be skewed against African languages. It is difficult to find such auto-complete suggestions in most languages in Africa. This also buttresses the need for indigenous digital systems that accommodate African languages. These anomalies can be corrected when African tech experts choose to be actively involved in algorithm development. If tech companies also review their recruitment processes to ensure adequate representation without compromising the desire for competence, it would also partly resolve certain intercultural gaps.

People's contexts can differ, and algorithms should not be developed in a way that is blind to peculiarities. One of the points AI developers must note in the attainment of singularity is the existence of humans living in different societies, having different norms. In 2016, the DeepMind AlphaGo programme made the news after defeating Lee Sedol in a board game (Yang et al., 2024, p. 2). We are not aware if AlphaGo could also solve other traditional games that would require the players to predict each other's next moves. By that, it also means that a player would have to be in the mind of the other. For a game that is played consecutively like Chinese and Japanese 'Go' and African 'mancala' games, it is easy to predict that an algorithmically inspired robot could be developed to win on all fronts.

What about a game that could be played simultaneously, mind-reading trick games and so on? In that case, to what extent could an algorithm be developed to respond to the accurate movements of a human agent? Possibly, this could happen if we distort the features of the human agent to respond to an algorithm. In such a situation, people would no longer be human but an artificially wired human agents. Within this realm, we could also have spiritual mediums, telepathy and other suprasensible activities that might be beyond the comprehension of DeepMind. All these are concerns that emanate from different backgrounds and influence the life worlds of different societies. If it works for some people, it cannot be dismissed as useless simply because it is beyond the scope of the most recent experimental science. AI systems should be enabled to understand different contexts and adapt their decision-making accordingly. At the same time, we believe that the responsibility to domesticate AI lies in the hands of developing nations that are in a disadvantaged position.

6.6 Conclusion

This discussion set out as a quest for justifiable governance for AI in Africa. We started by interrogating the concept of moral justice, where an effort was made to identify the inadequacies in the Western perspective that prioritises freedom and autonomy. Examining the African conception of justice, we noticed a more robust understanding that stresses the interconnectedness of people and prioritises our shared humanity in describing justice. We maintained that such a conception could help overcome potential dangers associated with AI governance. While different principles are often suggested for AI governance, the need for human oversight was stressed as a major principle. We observed that in Africa, there is a big deficit gap in global AI governance and argued for the integration of cultural diversities and the promotion of interculturality in the development of AI algorithms. By this, we could make use of the stimulating properties of interconnectedness in the African conception of justice as a more reliable defence and justifiable governance for AI in Africa.

References

Al Mutawa, M. A. (2009, May 12). Major powers seek to maintain superiority. *Gulf News*. https://www.pressreader.com/uae/gulf-news/20090512/281805689882242

Aquinas, T. (1947). *Summa Theologica* (Fathers of the English Dominican Province, Trans.). Benziger Brothers. (Original work published 1265–1274)

Azenabor, G. (2022). Omoluabi: An African conception of moral value. *Thought and Practice: A Journal of the Philosophical Association of Kenya*, *8*(2), 63–81.

Batool, A., Zowghi, D., & Bano, M. (2025). AI governance: A systematic literature review. *AI and Ethics*. https://doi.org/10.1007/s43681-024-00653-w

Beloume, A. (2023, February 28). The problems of internet privacy and big tech companies. *The Science Survey*. https://thesciencesurvey.com/news/2023/02/28/the-problems-of-internet-privacy-and-big-tech-companies/

Birhane, A. (2020). Algorithmic colonization of Africa. *Scripted*, *17*(2), 389–409. https://doi.org/10.2966/scrip.170220.389

Carr, S. (2024, April 18). Reporter's notebook: Even the 'father of IQ tests' thought the results weren't written in stone. *The Hechinger Report*. https://hechingerreport.org/reporters-notebook-even-the-father-of-iq-tests-thought-the-results-werent-written-in-stone/

Chonka, P., Diepeveen, S., & Haile, Y. (2023). Algorithmic power and African indigenous languages: Search engine autocomplete and the global multilingual internet. *Media, Culture & Society*, *45*(2), 246–265. https://doi.org/10.1177/01634437221104705

Coleman, D. (2019). Digital colonialism: The 21st-century scramble for Africa through the extraction and control of user data and the limitations of data protection laws, *Michigan Journal of Race and Law*, *24*, 417–439. https://doi.org/10.36643/mjrl.24.2.digital

Dietz, G. (2018). Interculturality. In H. Callan (Ed.), *The international encyclopedia of anthropology* (pp. 1–19). Wiley. https://doi.org/10.1002/9781118924396.wbiea1629

European Insurance and Occupational Pensions Authority. (2021). *Artificial intelligence governance principles: Towards ethical and trustworthy artificial intelligence in the European insurance sector*. Publication Office of the European Union.

Findley, B. (2020). Why racial bias is prevalent in facial recognition technology. *Harvard Journal of Law & Technology Digest*. https://jolt.law.harvard.edu/digest/why-racial-bias-is-prevalent-in-facial-recognition-technology

Ger, N., Lugossy, A.-M., & Petrucka, P. (2024). Status of "African research and its contribution to global health research: A review and an opinion." *Discover Public Health*, *21*(192). https://doi.org/10.1186/s12982-024-00323-6

Ghaffary, S. (2019, August 15). The algorithms that detect hate speech online are biased against Black people. *Vox*. https://www.vox.com/recode/2019/8/15/20806384/social-media-hate-speech-bias-black-african-american-facebook-twitter

Goodyear, S. (2023, May 4). The 'godfather of AI' says he's worried about 'the end of people.' *CBC Radio*. https://www.cbc.ca/amp/1.6830857

Gunaratna, S. (2017, March 13). Web inventor Tim Berners-Lee on the biggest problems with the internet today. *CBS News*. https://www.cbsnews.com/news/web-inventor-tim-berners-lee-biggest-problems-internet-fake-news-privacy/

Hauge, J. (2024, June 17). The free trade myth: How the US manipulates global markets for economic supremacy. *The Conversation*. https://theconversation.com/the-free-trade-myth-how-the-us-manipulates-global-markets-for-economic-supremacy-231609

Hendrix, J. (2025, February 2). The dangerous combination of technology and capitalism. *Tech Policy Press*. https://www.techpolicy.press/the-dangerous-combination-of-technology-and-capitalism/

Hoffman, J. (2023, February 14). Big Tech makes billions off our personal data. It's time for the US to pull in the reins. *Chicago Tribune*. https://www.chicagotribune.com/2023/02/14/jane-hoffman-big-tech-makes-billions-off-our-personal-data-its-time-for-the-us-to-pull-in-the-reins/

Kahn, M. J. (2022). The status of science, technology, and innovation in Africa. *Science, Technology and Society*, *27*(3), 327–350. https://doi.org/10.1177/09717218221078540

Kant, I. (1994). *Ethical philosophy: Grounding for the metaphysics of morals* (J. Ellington, Trans.). Hackett Publishing. (Original work published 1785)

Kastoryano, R. (2018). Multiculturalism and interculturalism: Redefining nationhood and solidarity. *Comparative Migration Studies*, *6*(17). https://doi.org/10.1186/s40878-018-0082-6

Lehdonvirta, V., Wú, B., & Hawkins, Z. (2024). Compute North vs. Compute South: The uneven possibilities of compute-based AI governance around the globe. Proceedings of the Seventh AAAI/ACM Conference on AI, Ethics, and Society (AIES 2024), 828–838. https://doi.org/10.31235/osf.io/8yp7z

Leyva, K. (2025). Fukuyama on politics, rights, and recognition. *Politics and Rights Review*. https://politicsrights.com/Fukuyama-on-politics-rights-and-recognition

Lindemann, B. (2023). The first wave of feminism: A movement created by and for Americans. *Journal of Student Research*, *12*(4), 1–5. https://doi.org/10.47611/jsrhs.v12i4.5637

Little, B. (2023, January 31). When Oppenheimer, 'father of the atomic bomb,' was blacklisted. *History*. https://www.history.com/news/father-of-the-atomic-bomb-was-blacklisted-for-opposing-h-bomb

Liu, L. (2024, January 8). Multicultural, cross-cultural, & intercultural. *London Intercultural Centre*. https://londoninterculturalcenter.co.uk/blogs/f/multicultural-cross-cultural-intercultural

Lu, E. (2020, June 5). Tech capitalism: Good or bad? *Forbes*. https://www.forbes.com/councils/forbesbusinesscouncil/2020/06/05/tech-capitalism-good-or-bad/

Lutz, D. (2024). Ubuntu, liberal individualism, and justice. In P. Nnodim & A. Okigbo (Eds.), *Ubuntu: A comparative study of an African concept of justice (pp.* 31–38*)*. Leuven University Press.

Maryville University. (2020, May 28). The evolution of social media: How did it begin, and where could it go next? https://online.maryville.edu/blog/evolution-social-media/

McNeilly, M. (2023). The human rights risks of artificial intelligence (AI). *New Tactics in Human Rights*. https://www.newtactics.org/perspectives/human-rights-risks-artificial-intelligence-ai/

Mill, J. S. (1863). *Utilitarianism*. Parker, Son, and Bourn.

Mpemba, C., & Munyati, C. (2023, August 16). How Africa's youth will drive global growth. *World Economic Forum*. https://www.weforum.org/stories/2023/08/africa-youth-global-growth-digital-economy/

Mucci, T. (2024, October 10). What is AI governance? *IBM*. https://www.ibm.com/think/topics/ai-governance

National Women's History Museum. (2021, April 5). Feminism: The first wave. *Women's History*. https://www.womenshistory.org/exhibits/feminism-first-wave-0

Ojimba, C. (2018). The concept of justice and its appeal to some theories in jurisprudence: An overview. *Journal of Commercial and Property Law*, *1*(1), 281–287.

Plato (2007). *The Republic* (Lee, D., Trans., 2nd ed.). Penguin Books. (Original work published c. 380 BCE)

Rabin-Havt, A., & Media Matters in America. (2016). *Lies, incorporated: The world of post-truth politics*. Anchor Books.

Sadowski, J. (2016, August 31). Companies are making money from our personal data – but at what cost? *The Guardian*. https://www.theguardian.com/technology/2016/aug/31/personal-data-corporate-use-google-amazon

Salami, A. O. (2024). Artificial intelligence, digital colonialism, and the implications for Africa's future development. *Data and Policy*, *6*(e67), 1–12. https://doi.org/10.1017/dap.2024.75

Sarwari, A. Q., Javed, M. N., Adnan, H. M., & Wahab, M. N. A. (2024). Assessment of the impacts of artificial intelligence (AI) on intercultural communication among postgraduate students in a multicultural university environment. *Scientific Reports*, *14*(13849). https://doi.org/10.1038/s41598-024-63276-5

Schulze, E. (2019, March 11). The man who invented the web says it's now dysfunctional with 'perverse' incentives. *CNBC*. https://www.cnbc.com/2019/03/11/tim-berners-lee-the-web-is-dysfunctional-with-perverse-incentives.html

Teleanu, S., & Kurbalija, J. (Lead authors). (2022). *Stronger digital voices from Africa: Building African digital foreign policy and diplomacy*. DiploFoundation.

Tidy, J. (2021, July 16). How your personal data is being scraped from social media. *BBC News*. https://www.bbc.com/news/business-57841239

United Nations Educational, Scientific and Cultural Organization. (2024, February 5). How intercultural dialogue can power peace? *Vision of Humanity*. https://www.visionofhumanity.org/how-intercultural-dialogue-can-power-peace/

Yang, S., Zhao, H., & Luo, W. (2024). The impact of artificial intelligence on intercultural communication. *IntechOpen*. https://doi.org/10.5772/intechopen.1006172

Zhu, H., Wei, D. D., Brandt, A., Chen, G., Ferri, G., Hazel, S., Jenks, C., Jones, R., O'Regan, J., & Suzuki, S. (2024). Exploring AI for intercultural communication: Open conversation. *Applied Linguistics Review*, 1–16. https://doi.org/10.1515/applirev-2024-0186

Zuboff, S. (2019). *The age of surveillance capitalism*. Public Affairs.

7 African Ubuntu, relational being and AI

Parker Robinson and Dorine van Norren

7.1 Introduction

In this chapter, we investigate the implicit underlying modernist economic ideology[1] behind artificial intelligence (AI) deployment in social roles that guide technologies, considering the role of humans in the economy (mainly as a production factor). We look at modernist understandings of the economy such as the commitment to infinite growth, the centering of individual flourishing, markets promoting the idea that self-interest will lead to collective welfare, and material wellbeing that often goes at the expense of natural surroundings. We argue that this modernist ideology denies the metaphysical (spiritual, religious dimensions of life) as well as the dependence that individual persons have on their communities and therefore diminishes our ability to flourish as human beings (Van Norren, 2020). To this end, we take a decolonial, intercultural view,[2] recognizing the dominance of Western systems of knowledge production and reasoning that are often portrayed to be of superior or sole value. To counter the exploitation of people and resources that are promoted by the supremacy of pervasive Western economic thought, we offer the perspective of the philosophy of Ubuntu, demonstrating the viability of a valid alternative to the individualist basis for AI development.

On the one hand, AI has brought many opportunities. AI may be beneficial for increasing productivity, taking over tedious and unfulfilling tasks from humans (G20, 2019; Van Norren, 2022, p. 10) and increasing emotional and physical comfort in its users (Prescott & Robillard, 2021). However, there are several risks associated with AI and robotic development as well, namely, the potential to exacerbate current social ills like inequality, bias, and, for social robots, to deceive and degrade social relations (G20, 2019; Sparrow & Sparrow, 2006; Van Norren 2023, p. 10).

This chapter delves into how current AI (robots using large language models) deployment into social roles may largely echo the current capitalist economy's hegemonic value system with respect to social relations. The model seems to largely see deficient social relations as a problem to be solved through the implementation of AI into social roles (Fiske & Buyx, 2023). The

DOI: 10.4324/9781003688853-9

"social role" is already a shifting definition, as many traditional social roles have been transitioned into paid occupations such as childcare, education, and nursing. In this sense, today's society has forgotten that these occupations were once assumed by members of one's direct community. Their purpose has been altered away from the care that is integral to them and toward the payment one receives for doing that care. As voluntary care work is not economically rewarded, it is often not considered as valuable. For example, this leads to the curious contradiction that taking care of one's own children does not count as productive work in the economic system but taking care of other people's children does. Caregiving is often no longer a *human* role, but a job. This alienates the occupants of these roles not only from their work but also from the relationships that they would otherwise form while in them. Caring for another *for the sake of the other* is an essentially human aspect of social roles, so when this motive shifts toward profit, the role becomes less human.

Moreover, reciprocity in relationships means that receiving care is equally as valuable as giving care. Companies developing AI often use language that characterizes our own human faculties as burdensome and basic human needs and abilities as things to be alleviated. For example, Turing, a software development company, has released an advertisement that reads "We train AI to think, reason, and code, so you don't have to, don't worry they're fast learners" (Turing, 2024). Abby (2024), a company rolling out "AI therapists," describes their product as "providing much-needed companionship and mental health support" to the elderly. Essential human practices are labeled as problems in need of fixing for the sake of efficiency, and crucially, AI is suited to solve them more efficiently, seemingly making human intervention redundant. This omits the value that is found in the *process* of care and relationships and is part of neoliberal thinking that instrumentalizes human activity to totality that has become very prevalent.

This chapter demonstrates that the implementation of AI into social roles is a consequence of:

1 the dominant view of the capitalist, profit-driven economy projected onto humans, leading to the impoverishment of social networks in the industrialized world (United Kingdom Department for Culture, Media and Sport, [UKDCMS], 2024; Gallup, 2023; Pew Research Center, 2023; Kannan & Veazie, 2022);
2 the pernicious and dominant underlying modernist assumption that social relations exist solely to fulfill the desires and interests of individuals or that of the economy (Ntibagirirwa, 2012; Polanyi, 1944/2001) and that personhood is individual and not social (Douglas & Ney, 1998);
3 the neocolonial omission of non-Western value systems when considering the ethics of AI—despite worldwide efforts by United Nations Educational, Scientific and Cultural Organization (UNESCO) to draw up guidelines for the ethics of AI (Van Norren, 2023)—forming an epistemic injustice (leaving aside that some may also consider UNESCO a neo-colonial institution).

Part of epistemic justice is considering multiple knowledge systems when solving problems, particularly those of the groups affected by these problems (Bhambra, 2021; Cummings et al., 2023; Fricker, 2007; Mungwini, 2018; Tobi, 2022). Contrary to the often-heard objection that this confuses things too much and makes truth elusive and relative, multiple knowledge systems enrich the debate by offering more than one solution or perspective, rather than diluting "truth" (in other words: the dominant view imposed by colonial Western powers gives an adequate representation of the truth rather than hiding its exploitative nature and obliterating other cultures' and people's point of view and experience of exploitation). Hence, epistemic justice (knowledge system equality) is required. Epistemic justice compels us to refocus technological development that will inevitably affect people and cultures across the globe, by thus building its foundation on decolonial, non-exploitative, intercultural systems of thought.

The sub-Saharan African philosophy of Ubuntu offers a contrasting idea of social roles and their relation to personhood (Metz & Gaie, 2010), one that acknowledges the relational and processual nature of being (Menkiti, 1984). Not only is there a moral imperative to upend the unilateral dominance of hegemonic Western thought, the results of purely relying on a Western ideology in AI implementation may be cause for concern when implemented in or imposed upon non-Western societies, reinforcing already existing trends in Western or industrialized societies of loneliness and fragmentation (Blackpool et al., 2018; UK Department for Culture, Media and Sport, UKDCMS, 2023). This is especially true when looking at AI deployment into social roles, as AI risks amplifying the current biases of a (Western-based) global society whose highest good is the freedom of the individual rather than mutual aid. Communitarian value systems such as Ubuntu offer a picture of humanity that may aid in restoring communal relations and stopping further fragmentation of our communities and selves.

7.2 Methodology

We begin by analyzing the current implementation of AI into public roles, specifically focusing on their deployment into roles characterized by the giving and receiving of care, or what we will call *social roles*. We will then analyze the underlying logic of our current capitalist economic thinking that creates the context in which we employ technologies such as AI into these roles. The premises are based on enlightenment thinking that created today's (modernist) take on society as epitomized in neoliberal economics: we are atomic individuals who associate with one another out of voluntary self-interest; we emphasize rights and freedoms rather than duties and boundedness to one another; we are material(ist), rational, competitive beings; and we are production factors in the economy along with natural resources rather than seeking meaning in the activities of life, now called work; we are above nature and treat it as an object rather than a subject (Ntibagirirwa, 2012; Van Norren, 2017); Wells, 2010).

To show that another account of humanity, economy, and AI is possible, and in many ways preferable, we take an intercultural decolonial view of society inspired by post-colonial economics and philosophy by introducing the African Ubuntu view of the moral person. The philosophy of Ubuntu allows us to understand the role of humans in society and the injustices that occur when AI occupy roles in our communities. We do so to restore other knowledge systems that have long been ignored and degraded and use epistemic justice (Bhambra, 2021; Van Norren, 2023) to evaluate current developments.

7.3 Modernist foundations of "Social AI"

The rapid deployment of AI into everyday life can illuminate how those developing and deploying these machines and programs, such as diagnostic programs and care-bots, view them and the roles they are made to occupy. In the medical field, AI is often used to identify health conditions and suggest effective remedies for patients (Al-Antari, 2023). When one deploys an AI to analyze medical patients' conditions, this part of the role of the doctor is treated as a technical problem that an AI is capable of solving. Diagnosing medical conditions, transportation optimization, and other data analysis problems can all be categorized mainly as *technical problems*.

We will imagine *technical problems* as problems that are clearly defined, can be measured, and solved through a goal-oriented process (Polanyi, 1944/2001). We can imagine these problems being evaluated in terms of how effective they are at bringing about the intended state of affairs. These seem to implore the implementation of AI and, in many cases, render an effective contribution to efficiency. Technical problems are essential components of social roles but are not fully encompassing of those roles. We should understand *social problems* as distinct from technical problems, in that they necessarily involve the process of interpersonal care and interpersonal connection. Elderly care, childhood development, therapy, nursing, and many others are roles that may fall under this label. AI implementation into these social roles illuminates the underlying ideology that permeates AI development and deployment practices.

AI is only the most recent step in a long line of the professionalization and commodification of *social roles,* such as therapists, professional childcare workers, and elderly home workers (Bruhn & Rebach, 2014). Dissimilar to other forms of economic pressure on social roles that treat the care involved in them as a mere means to the end of profit, the introduction of AI through economic forces redefines care entirely. The act of caring by humans itself is seen as just another (and less efficient) means to accomplish the task of, for example, relieving the pain of the patient. In this sense, the humanity involved in caring becomes a nonessential, or even an obsolete, part of social roles and human life.

The commodification of care and the occupation of social roles by AI are fueled by the underlying modernist ideology of individualism. Western conceptions of personhood center around autonomy, the individual, rationality, freedom, rights, capabilities (actualizing one's rights), and the capitalist drive to ascend from the masses to a status above others (Van Norren, 2020). These views contain a strong libertarian ideal (Smith, 1776) as echoed by the prominent conservative politician, Margaret Thatcher, "Who is society? There is no such thing! There are individual men and women and there are families, and no government can do anything except through people and people look to themselves first" (Thatcher, 1987a). This sentiment offers a view that communities and the relationships that make up such a network are the product of self-interested, atomic individuals voluntarily associating with one another. Society is meant to be conceived solely as an aggregation of individual, material human beings (Menkiti, 1984).

The modernist view, therefore, paints a deflationary picture of the metaphysical weight of relationships, viewing them only as ways in which persons stand in relation to one another and not as *constitutive* of these persons. The view omits not only the metaphysical substance of human relations but their normative significance as well, in the sense that to become a full moral person, one must be socialized and incorporated into the community and culture around them. Relationships are described simply as means to one's own personal end(s), rendering them replaceable by any other sufficient means. Relationships give rise to no more meaning than a hammer does for a carpenter: they are functional rather than meaning generating. In a similar vein, work is not considered an activity giving meaning to one's life but a necessary productive force for the (capitalist) economy. Post-colonial economic thinkers going beyond (neo)colonial capitalist exploitative systems, include the degrowth movement pleading for zero growth or no longer using the concept of growth (D'Alisa et al., 2014) and they include those who call for the downscaling of growth economies toward sustainable models of society (Weiss & Cattaneo, 2017). They concur with those decolonial thinkers who plead for restoring the central role of humans in society and the sovereignty of humans and nature over capital from the point of view of Ubuntu and Latin American Buen Vivir (Good Living) (Acosta, 2015; Ramose, 1999/2005).

There is an implicit and consistent view in the tech world, as gleaned through their public statements and marketing efforts (see, e.g., statements from companies like Abby, ElliQ, IBM, and Turing), that almost any activity that humans engage in can and should be "solved." Working, thinking, and creating are often viewed as burdens to be alleviated or tasks that are becoming inefficient for humans to continue doing, given the advent of AI, at least when it comes to distributing AI as a product.[3] This view is especially concerning when it guides the deployment of pseudo-social AI into social roles. Abby, a company focused on developing "AI therapists," explains the goal of their product as follows: "AI therapy represents a promising tool in our efforts to combat loneliness among the elderly, providing much-needed companionship and mental health support" (Abby, 2024). Here, Abby paints companionship as a relationship that is possible to exist in without other persons. They are under no illusion that their chat-bot is not sentient, is not a person, and yet they posit that it is capable of providing "much-needed companionship" (Abby, 2024). Abby's characterization of companionship treats it as more similar to a mental state than to a metaphysically real relationship. The *social role* of elderly care is reduced to a *technical role*—the task of removing the elder's pain entailed in loneliness.

Abby's rhetoric surrounding their product is reflective of more than the company's tactics for achieving sales. Another technology company, ElliQ, that has successfully brought AI "companions" to market shares some of its users' testimony on its website (for more on the development of ElliQ, see Broadbent et al., 2024). Seniors are recorded as saying that ElliQ is "the best friend you could ever have"; "she is in fact, a companion"; and "she cares about me, and makes sure I'm doing okay" (ElliQ, n.d.).

This deception goes beyond the common anthropomorphizing of inanimate objects that we are attached to and illuminates deeper mistakes (Sparrow & Sparrow, 2006); these testimonies reflect the deeper omission and deception about what we owe to our elderly (and to ourselves) as well as the value of human relationships. The meaning that is often found in relationships like companionship is forgotten in favor of a model of relationships that can be tapped by economic markets.

The markets have brought with them benefits to social roles as well. AI, being able to access much larger data sets, may be able to recognize behavioral patterns in patients who may have gone overlooked otherwise (Zhou et al., 2021). They face other problems though, such as bias, often stemming from skewed data sets (Cowgill et al., 2020) and the possibility to replace instead of simply supplementing social occupations (Brandes & Wattenhofer, 2024).

7.4 Ubuntu ethics, relational personhood, and its significance for the economy

The integration of multiple knowledge systems (epistemologies) as an alternative ethic to the capitalist economic ideology currently predominantly driving the general economic logic and thus AI development is imperative. AI ethics guidelines are primarily developed in the West while AI is implemented around the world, and currently, the Western ethical, human rights-centered view dominates (Van Norren, 2023). Although this is not necessarily negative, it may overlook certain aspects such as the communal. The UNESCO recommendation on the ethics of AI was the first worldwide attempt to draw up AI ethics guidelines. This view centers around general human rights principles, inclusiveness, flourishing (leaving unclear whether this is individual or communal), alongside accountability, autonomy, democracy, explainability, good governance, literacy, responsibility, transparency, and sustainability (UNESCO World Commission on the Ethics of Scientific Knowledge and Technology [COMEST], 2019), but as Van Norren (2023) demonstrates largely leaves out Other epistemologies from the Global South such as Ubuntu.

The Ubuntu ethic is one founded in the movement of life, the inherent dependence on life around us, and the affirmation of change. Ifeanyi Menkiti and Mogobe Ramose (among others) developed the oral tradition of Ubuntu into a language "familiar to modern philosophy" (Menkiti, 1984, p. 171; Ramose, 1999/2005; see also e.g., Eze, 2010; Gade, 2012; Metz & Gaie, 2010), building on earlier writers such as Mbiti (1969/1990). Menkiti explains the African conception of human beings as a *processual* and *relational* existence so that persons exist in light of their community, not the other way around. Therefore, one often refers to the adage: a person is a person through other persons (Mbiti, 1969/1990, Ramose, 1999/2005) (concurring with some Western post-modernist conceptions). Personhood, in other words, is social, as these Western scientists have also argued (Douglas & Ney, 1998, p. 124). The African Ubuntu view of personhood (which resonates throughout Africa), as contrasted with the current dominant Western individualist view, is that personhood is not a fixed status that one inherits when one is born. Instead, personhood exists on a gradient scale that depends on moral behavior and the development of ethical relationships within one's community. Crucially, these relationships do not exist merely as voluntary associations between individuals but necessarily and prior to the development of personhood: language, reason, and other cognitive processes often deemed as essential for personhood are developed only because of one's participation in a group (Ogude, 2018). Moral personhood describes the development and incorporation of an individual into the community, which one acquires by normative behavior and can also lose by aberrative behavior. Ubuntu's concept of justice is one of restoration of relationships within the community; hence, restorative justice is preferred over punitive justice (Eze, 2010).

Everything in the Ubuntu philosophy is geared toward harmonious, reciprocal (and non-exploitative) relationships within society and with one's natural surroundings from the belief that we are all interconnected and inherently interdependent (Behrens, 2010; Ramose, 1999/2005; Metz, 2007). This is highlighted most prominently in the attention given to intergenerational learning between young and old (Padayachee et al., 2022). To demonstrate their importance in the community, children were also involved in decision-making processes (Mayaka & Truell, 2021, p. 653). The community consists of the ancestors, the current generation, and the future generation: they form the community of now (Van Norren, 2020). Individuals find themselves intertwined into these communal networks not only relying on them but also being called on to tend to them. In this way, all people have a duty to care for the world around them and the beings that constitute this world.

Ubuntu's view on the economy places the human and their communities in the center. Ubuntu holds sharing and caring for the other as the core principles of life. From this, Ramose (1999/2005) criticizes the sovereignty of capital and the economy over humans. In this sense, the dominant economic structure treats care as subordinate to profit, only seeing it as a means to the end of wealth accumulation. Moreover, in the Ubuntu philosophy, the essence of work is not merely providing a means of living, but in itself creates meaning in life. Work is not done for a profit, but as an essential feature of being human, working-as-one in the community (shosholoza), caring, exchanging, producing, sharing food, and other necessities in providing basic needs along with developing one's abilities and expressing oneself, creating beauty, and enhancing life itself. Money is only a means to an end and must be treated as such (Louw, 1998; Ramose, 1999/2005).

These acts of communal engagement and care are not only activities undertaken in order to improve the life of the people receiving the care but also are essential for the *carer* themselves, in that providing care constitutes meaning as much as receiving care. Acts of care are essential to developing into a full person and are a central source of meaning in one's life. From Ubuntu's logic that reciprocity should drive healthy human relations, we can then derive healthy economic, legal, and governance relations (Van Norren, 2025).

7.5 Social AI, the reduction of personhood and ontological harm

The pervasiveness of the individualist, capitalist worldview has allowed for AI to be implemented into roles that would have been thought unimaginable for them to occupy previously. Ubuntu offers a framework for understanding the deep harm that AI implementation may do to "being" itself (ontological harm), if continually propelled by a singular and impoverished worldview centered around profit and efficiency.

AI deployment into social roles may harm those whom the AI are meant to assist by replacing relationships with a robotic simulation and removing uniquely human qualities of interaction. Ubuntu allows us to see that the replacement of relationships, such as for the elderly, diminishes their ability to remain incorporated in their communities and play the meaningful role of contributing to the development of the younger generation. In the absence of elderly figures in their communities, youths' ability to become a full person through this care exchange is hampered. Thus, this solution may create another problem—namely, depression and a sense of redundancy among elders. Sonnenberg (2020), for example, demonstrates this in the modernization of mediation practices previously carried out by the elderly in Bhutan. The elderly, in the Ubuntu view, are the most full and revered persons. By maturing, they have not simply "take[n] on additional features, [but] under[gone] fundamental changes at the core of one's being" (Menkiti, 1984, p. 173). Where a Western conception of personhood may see old people as diminished persons because they have weakened rational capacity and no longer contribute to economic development, Ubuntu sees them as having developed in moral persons more fully than younger generations. They therefore have the ability to contribute substantially to society, a fact overlooked in the modern capitalist view (Van Norren, 2023). The robotization of care may harm both the elderly and the young, as well as the mature productive population, by severing the relationships between those developing into full persons and those at the end of their development.

In the case of childcare, AI implementation into the roles of educators would be devastating in the Ubuntu view for the same reason that isolating the elderly would be. Children are the least developed people and therefore the most in need of communal relationships, especially with those who can act as mentors, guiding them to become full persons. Children must acquire a sense of self through their connectedness with their community and develop a sense of duty to those around them. To fully flourish as a human being, one must *continually become* by "fulfilling [their] role in the community" (Van Norren, 2023, p. 117). The elderly are not only denied true, reciprocal friendship, but their full personhood, and even more so are the young since they are at the start of their life.

The elderly may also become diminished as moral persons by being rendered moral patients. Chimakonam (2024) develops the view that if AI systems can be rational agents, there is a possibility that they can surpass the human capacity for moral autonomy and thereby dominate human beings. If AI have the potential to significantly surpass us as moral agents in their capacity for moral reasoning, they may render us moral patients, removing our agency and diminishing our moral status (Chimakonam, 2024). However, the fear of humans being reduced to mere moral patients should arise earlier in the stages of AI development. The elderly are unable to *act* as moral agents if they only interact with inanimate AI: they are only able to be acted upon by AI that cannot be considered agents yet. Caring, or more broadly fulfilling one's associational duties, is essential to the relationships one holds: not simply being cared for by others but caring for others as well.

As Ubuntu illuminates for us, the degradation of communities is destructive to the individual person as well. It is not physical destruction, however, but an internal one. The reduced ability to incorporate oneself into a community reduces our ability to be persons (Menkiti, 1984); traversing and integrating oneself through and into the social landscape of a community is part of what it means to be a person. This conception of personhood provides a picture that contrasts with mainstream Western accounts, in which, by possessing the qualities of a rational will, capacity for autonomy and moral agency, one is a person. Ubuntu does not deny that moral agency is integral to personhood but contrasts with Western views, in that it views moral agency not as a static quality reducible to mental capacities but as a status born out of continual commitment to the flourishing of one's relationships and community.

7.6 Conclusion

In this chapter, we discussed the ethical implications of AI deployment into social roles. We broke down the underlying individualist ideology guiding current AI implementation in these roles and offered the philosophy of Ubuntu to account for its potential harms to individuals and communities. We did this through the lens of both post-colonialism and post-colonial economics and epistemic justice.

The processual nature of personhood, accounted for by the Ubuntu philosophy, should urge us to focus on the different kinds of relations between humans and AI. In the case of AI being implemented into social roles, existing communities (and community spirit) can be degraded. The deployment of AI in, among others, the role of "elderly-companion," in medical diagnosis roles influencing the doctor-patient relationship, and in educational roles, seems to be accepted mainly through adherence to Western ideals of individual personhood, and a strong capitalist pull toward transactional relationships. The idea that an AI can act as a companion necessitates a teleological (goal-oriented as developed through our conception of *technical problems* and result-based thinking) understanding of companionship such that the role of a companion is to achieve some state of the world. In the case of elderly care, the goal of this association is the alleviation of the pain intrinsic to loneliness. Ubuntu rejects the claim that communities are merely "aggregated sums of individuals" (Eze, 2010; Mbiti, 1969/1990; Menkiti, 1984, p. 179; Metz & Gaie, 2010; Ntibagirirwa, 2012; Ramose, 1999/2005). The aforementioned African authors argue that communities are more than mere associations, that they are the basis for personhood. Communities and social relations are not something to be accomplished; they are the root of personhood, the root of an individual's existence, and way of being in the world that cannot be ignored.

The insertion of AI into a social role not only further isolates one from one's own humanity but also eliminates that role, which a human could have flourished in and created meaning from. When we look at social roles from a teleological point of view, treating social roles simply as technical challenges, it starts to seem reasonable to allow AI to occupy these roles in our communities (or lack thereof). But as Ubuntu tells us, one's relationships are not valuable because they fulfill some set of desires but because they are themselves necessary for personhood and that interconnection and interdependence are the essence of being human. All human roles are social roles because to be human is to be social! The implementation of AI into occupations inherently treats social aspects of occupations as inefficient human residue to be reduced in the name of efficiency. AI's entrenchment in the Western, profit-oriented economic regime means that any exhibition of human behavior is only developed to the extent that it is necessary to make humans tolerant of them. Can entities that are created to fulfill a list of tasks ever enter true relationships? Moreover, the large-scale deployment of AI without careful consideration of multiple cultural knowledge systems risks exacerbating already existing flaws (and biases) of the current economic and social systems in industrialized countries without knowing it (Gallup, 2023; Pew Research Center, 2023; Kannan & Veazie, 2022; (UK Department for Culture, Media and Sport UKDCMS, 2024;).

In our rapidly developing and increasingly interconnected world, the adherence to a single worldview causing epistemic injustice is not only arrogant but also dangerous. The colonization of the global system of knowledge reduces our view of humanity to a singular understanding, which is unlikely to be an all-encapsulating vantage point. This requires us to actively consider alternative conceptions of personhood and human experience to achieve a fuller picture of who we are as humans. As Ubuntu shows us, this epistemic injustice leads to ontological harm: as our communities and relationships are degraded, our ability to become full moral persons diminishes.

Not only can a view like Ubuntu offer a framework for centering our humanity and interconnectedness in AI development instead of ostracizing and depleting it, it also offers an account of the root of current psychological afflictions (depression, loneliness, etc.) as being seated in the purposelessness and alienation that plague the jobs in modern economies and create room for a perceived need for social AI. Undoubtedly, AI will bring many benefits, but let us use those benefits carefully, reflecting on the role of humans in society and our desired relationship to technology.

Notes

1 A product of the European enlightenment and reaction to romanticism (Wells, 2010). See Adam Smith's *The Wealth of Nations* from 1776 and the 'invisible hand'—the idea that individuals rationally pursue their economic self-interest and that, in a free market, this serves the general good.

2 Interculturality denotes minimally "the recognition and inclusion of diversity" and more profoundly "opening of pathways towards a different society based on respect, mutual legitimacy, equity… where difference is the constitutive element" (Walsh, 2009, pp. 74 and 79).

3 "Imagine a world where machines aren't confined to pre-programmed tasks but operate with human-like autonomy and competence… But, unlike humans, AGIs don't experience fatigue or have biological needs and can constantly learn and process information at unimaginable speeds" (IBM, 2024, paras. 1 and 3).

References

Abby. (2024, June 17). *AI therapy as a companion for the elderly in assisted living*. https://abby.gg/mental-health/ai-therapy-as-a-companion-for-the-elderly-in-assisted-living/

Acosta, A. (2015). *Buen Vivir Vom Recht auf ein gutes Leben*. Friedrich Ebert Stiftung. Oekom Verlag.

Al-Antari, M. A. (2023). Artificial intelligence for medical diagnostics—Existing and future AI technology! *Diagnostics* 13(4), 688. https://doi.org/10.3390/diagnostics13040688

Behrens, K. (2010). Exploring African holism with respect to the environment. *Environmental Values*, *19*(4), 465–484. https://doi.org/10.3197/096327110X531552

Bhambra, G. K. (2021). Epistemic justice as a "new normal?" Interrogating the epistemic injustice of coloniality. *Sustainable Development*, *29*(5), 951–963. https://doi.org/10.1002/sd.3285

Blackpool, Gjovik, & Tokyo. (2018, September 1). Loneliness is a serious public-health problem *The Economist*. https://www.economist.com/international/2018/09/01/loneliness-is-a-serious-public-health-problem

Brandes, B., & Wattenhofer, R. (2024). Will AI replace human jobs? *PNAS Nexus*, *3*(6), 191. https://doi.org/10.1093/pnasnexus/pgae191

Broadbent, E., Loveys, K., Ilan, G., Chen, G., Chilukuri, M. M., Boardman, S. G., Doraiswamy, P. M., & Skuler, D. (2024). ElliQ, an AI-driven social robot to alleviate loneliness: Progress and lessons learned, *JAR Life*, *13*, 22–28. https://doi.org/10.14283/jarlife.2024.2

Bruhn, J. G., & Rebach, H. M. (2014). Social change and caregiving. In *The sociology of caregiving* (pp. 25–48). Springer. https://doi.org/10.1007/978-94-017-8857-1_2

Chimakonam, A. E. (2024). The ethics at the intersection of artificial intelligence and transhumanism: A personhood-based approach. *Data & Policy*, *6*, Article e61. https://doi.org/10.1017/dap.2024.59

Cowgill, B., Dell'Acqua, F., Deng, S., Hsu, D., Verma, N., & Chaintreau, A. (2020). Biased programmers? Or biased data? A field experiment in operationalizing AI ethics. *arXiv*. https://arxiv.org/abs/2012.02394

Cummings, S., Dhewa, C., Kemboi, G., & Young, S. (2023). Doing epistemic justice in sustainable development: Applying the philosophical concept of epistemic injustice to the real world. *Sustainable Development*, *31*(3), 453–462. https://doi.org/10.1002/sd.2497

D'Alisa, G. Demaria, F. Kallis, G. (Eds.). (2014). *Degrowth: A vocabulary for A new era*. Routledge.

Douglas, M., & Ney, S. (1998). *Missing persons: A critique of the social sciences*. University of California Press.

ElliQ. (n.d.). *Testimonials*. https://elliq.com/pages/testimonials

Eze, M. O. (2010). *Intellectual history of contemporary South Africa*. Palgrave Macmillan.

Fiske, A., & Buyx, A. (2023). Should artificial intelligence play a role in cultivating social connections among older adults? *AMA Journal of Ethics*, *25*(11), E839–E844. https://journalofethics.ama-assn.org/article/should-artificial-intelligence-play-role-cultivating-social-connections-among-older-adults/2023-11

Fricker, M. (2007). *Epistemic justice: Power and the politics of knowledge*. Oxford University Press.

G20. (2019). *G20 ministerial statement on trade and digital economy*. https://www.mofa.go.jp/files/000486596.pdf

Gade, C. B. N. (2012). What is Ubuntu? Different interpretations among South Africans of African descent. *South African Journal of Philosophy*, *31*(3), 484–503.

Gallup. (2023, December 13). *Almost a quarter of the world feels lonely, Meta-Gallup survey finds*. https://news.gallup.com/opinion/gallup/512618/almost-quarter-world-feels-lonely.aspx

IBM. (2024, April 18). *Artificial general intelligence examples*. https://www.ibm.com/think/topics/artificial-general-intelligence-examples

Kannan, V.D., & Veazie, P.J. (2022). US trends in social isolation, social engagement, and companionship - nationally and by age, sex, race/ethnicity, family income, and work hours, 2003-2020. *SSM - population health* vol. 21 101331. https://doi.org/10.1016/j.ssmph.2022.101331

Louw, D. J. (1998). *Ubuntu: An African assessment of the religious other*. Paper presented at the 20th World Congress of Philosophy, Boston, MA. http://www.bu.edu/wcp/Papers/Afri/AfriLouw.htm

Mayaka, B., & Truell, R. (2021). Ubuntu and its potential impact on the international social work profession. *International Social Work*, *64*(5), 649–662.

Mbiti, J. S. (1990). *African religions and philosophy* (2nd ed.). Heinemann Educational Publishers. (Original work published 1969)

Menkiti, I. A. (1984). Person and community in African traditional thought. In R. Wright (Ed.), *African philosophy: An introduction* (pp. 171–181). University Press of America.

Metz, T. (2007). Toward an African moral theory. *Journal of Political Philosophy*, *15*(3), 321–341. https://doi.org/10.1111/j.1467-9760.2007.00280.x

Metz, T., & Gaie, J. B. R. (2010). The African ethic of Ubuntu/Botho: Implications for research on morality. *Journal of Moral Education*, *39*(3), 273–290.

Mungwini, P. (2018). The question of epistemic justice: Polemics, contestations and dialogue. *Phronimon*, *19*, 1–13. https://doi.org/10.25159/2413-3086/3251

Ntibagirirwa, S. (2012). *Philosophical premises for African economic development: Sen's capability approach* (Doctoral dissertation). University of Pretoria.

Ogude, J. (Ed.). (2018). *Ubuntu and personhood*. Africa World Press. https://africaworldpressbooks.com/ubuntu-and-personhood-edited-by-james-ogude-1/

Padayachee, K., Maistry, S., Harris, G., & Lortan, D. (2022). Exploring the value of the Indigenous knowledge of Ubuntu in early childhood education in South Africa. *Africa Education Review*, *19*(3), 78–100. https://doi.org/10.1080/18146627.2023.2243379

Pew Research Center. (2023, December 6). *Connectedness to community, country, and the world*. https://www.pewresearch.org/global/2023/12/06/connectedness-to-community-country-and-the-world/

Polanyi, K. (2001). *The great transformation: The political and economic origins of our time*. Beacon Press. (Original work published 1944)

Prescott, T. J., & Robillard, J. M. (2021). Are friends electric? The benefits and risks of human-robot relationships. *iScience*, *24*, Article 101993. https://doi.org/10.1016/j.isci.2020.101993

Ramose, M. B. (2005). *African philosophy through Ubuntu* (Rev. ed.). Mond Books. (Original work published 1999)

Smith, A. (1776). *An inquiry into the nature and causes of the wealth of nations* (Vol. 1, Book I, Chapter II). Adam Black, William Tait, & Longman, Rees, Orme, Brown, & Green. http://gesd.free.fr/smith76bis.pdf

Sonnenberg, S. (2020). Formalizing the informal: Development and its impacts on traditional dispute resolution in Bhutan. *Washington University Journal of Law & Policy*, *63*(1), 143–206.

Sparrow, R., & Sparrow, L. (2006). In the hands of machines? The future of aged care. *Minds and Machines*, *16*(2), 141–161. https://doi.org/10.1007/s11023-006-9030-6

Thatcher, M. (1987a, September 23). *Interview for Woman's Own ("no such thing [as society]").*

Thatcher, M. (1987b). [Speech transcript]. Margaret Thatcher Foundation. https://www.margaretthatcher.org/document/106689

Tobi, A. (2022). Epistemic injustice and colonisation. *South African Journal of Philosophy*, *41*(4), 337–346. https://doi.org/10.1080/02580136.2023.2199605

Turing. (2024, March 25). *We train AGI to code, reason, and think, so you don't have to – don't worry, they're fast learners* [Image attached]. Instagram.

UNESCO-COMEST. (2019). *Preliminary study on the ethics of artificial intelligence.* UNESCO World Commission on the Ethics of Scientific Knowledge and Technology. https://unesdoc.unesco.org/ark:/48223/pf0000367823.

United Kingdom Department for Culture, Media and Sport. (2023). *Tackling loneliness annual report March 2023: The fourth year* [Policy paper]. UK Government. https://www.gov.uk/government/publications/loneliness-annual-report-the-fourth-year/tackling-loneliness-annual-report-march-2023-the-fourth-year

United Kingdom Department for Culture, Media and Sport. (2024). *Community Life Survey 2023/24: Civic engagement and social action*. UK Government. https://www.gov.uk/government/statistics/community-life-survey-202324-annual-publication/community-life-survey-202324-civic-engagement-and-social-action

Van Norren, D. E. (2017). Development as *service*. A *happiness*, Ubuntu and Buen Vivir interdisciplinary view of the Sustainable Development Goals [PhD Dissertation]. Tilburg university.

Van Norren, D. E. (2020). The sustainable development goals viewed through gross national happiness, ubuntu, and buen vivir. *International Environmental Agreements: Politics, Law and Economics*, *20*(3), 431–458. https://doi.org/10.1007/s10784-020-09487-3

Van Norren, D. E. (2023). The ethics of artificial intelligence, UNESCO and the African ubuntu perspective. *Journal of Information, Communication and Ethics in Society*, *21*(1), 112–128. https://doi.org/10.1108/JICES-04-2022-0037

Van Norren, D. E. (2025). *African Ubuntu and its view on law, human rights and sustainable development goals*. Cambridge Scholars.

Walsh, C. (2009). The Plurinational and Intercultural State: Decolonization and State Re-founding in Ecuador. *Kult 6 (Special Issue)*: 65-84 Roskilde University: Department of Culture and Identity. http://www.postkolonial.dk/artikler/kult_6/WALSH.pdf

Weiss, M., & Cattaneo, C. (2017). Degrowth: Taking stock and reviewing an emerging academic paradigm. *Ecological Economics*, *137*, 220–230. https://doi.org/10.1016/j.ecolecon.2017.01.014

Wells, W. (2010). Modernist economics. *Historically Speaking*, 11(5), 2–6. https://doi.org/10.1353/hsp.2010.a405433

Zhou, J., Lamichhane, B., Ben-Zeev, D., Campbell, A., & Sano, A. (2021). Routine clustering of mobile sensor data facilitates psychotic relapse prediction in schizophrenia patients. *arXiv*. https://arxiv.org/abs/2106.11487

8 Cultural futures

Governance, cultural policy and the political economy of AI in the Creative and Cultural Industries

Aziz Qaissi

8.1 Introduction

Governments worldwide are adapting their policy frameworks to capitalize on the transformative potential of AI, albeit in markedly different ways (Bullock et al., 2024; Srivastava & Bullock, 2024). Indeed, the incorporation of AI into policy frameworks has become a significant indicator of how governance structures are evolving in response to rapid technological change. These structures refer to the institutional arrangements, regulatory mechanisms, strategic policies, and administrative capacities that guide decision-making and public service delivery. An illustrative example is the *Government AI Readiness Index* (Oxford Insights, 2024), which evaluates how well-positioned governments are to deploy AI within public administration and service delivery. The index is structured around three foundational pillars: the public sector, the technology industry, and data and infrastructure. These categories encompass a range of criteria, including the presence of national AI strategies, investment levels in AI research and development, the maturity of digital infrastructure, and the establishment of ethical and regulatory safeguards. For instance, the UK government has deployed AI in healthcare through the National Health Service, using algorithms to predict patient wait times and optimize resource allocation (Devlin, 2019). However, concerns have been raised about biases in predictive tools, prompting calls for stricter oversight. Meanwhile, Estonia uses AI for public services like automated tax filing and chatbot-assisted legal advice (European Monitor of Industrial Ecosystems, 2020). Its success stems from strong digital infrastructure and proactive policy frameworks. In contrast, the United States has focused on AI in law enforcement, with cities like Los Angeles using predictive policing algorithms—a controversial approach criticized for reinforcing racial biases (Heaven, 2020).[1]

In the field of cultural policy, state approaches to governing the deployment of AI in Creative and Cultural Industries (CCIs) remain highly context-dependent, often marked by fragmentation and uneven development across regions. In advanced economies such as the European Union (EU), regulatory efforts like the EU AI Act (2024) have introduced sector-wide obligations

DOI: 10.4324/9781003688853-10

for transparency and accountability. However, these efforts are still evolving and have been critiqued for favoring corporate interests over creators' rights, particularly in areas such as copyright enforcement (Rankin, 2025). By contrast, many countries in the Global South are still formulating coherent digital and cultural policies that meaningfully address the intersection of AI and cultural production, constrained by limited institutional capacity and competing development priorities. Thus, while AI opens new possibilities for content creation, distribution, and audience engagement, the policy frameworks governing these transformations are often partial, reactive, and disproportionately influenced by the agendas of dominant technology firms. Copyright disputes, such as the *New York Times*' lawsuit against OpenAI (Grynbaum & Mac, 2023), reveal how AI models exploit cultural works without compensating creators, while labor conflicts like the Screen Actors Guild-American Federation of Television and Radio Artists (SAG-AFTRA) strikes highlight threats to artists' rights from AI replication tools (SAG-AFTRA, 2024).

In this chapter, the term culture refers broadly to the practices, institutions, values, and symbolic systems that shape how communities produce, interpret, and disseminate meaning. This definition encompasses a wide range of human activities, from the formal cultural industries—such as media, film, literature, music, and heritage—to the more informal, everyday cultural expressions embedded in daily life, such as language, rituals, traditions, and social practices. It also includes the policies, regulations, and institutional frameworks that govern and shape these activities, ranging from state-supported cultural initiatives to global market forces influencing local production and consumption. This conceptualization of culture positions it as both a site of identity formation and a locus of contestation, where competing narratives, values, and interests emerge and interact. Culture, in this sense, is not a static or monolithic entity but a dynamic and evolving field, deeply intertwined with technological advancements and political-economic structures. Technological change, such as the rise of digital media and new communication platforms, has dramatically altered how cultural products are produced, consumed, and shared, while the political economy—shaped by power relations, economic interests, and global forces—affects how cultural resources are distributed and whose voices are heard. As such, culture is not merely a reflection of society but an active force in shaping the social, political, and economic landscape.

In this context, cultural governance is understood as the broader mechanisms, institutions, and power relations through which cultural life is shaped, regulated, and contested. It encompasses not only formal, state-sanctioned interventions but also informal practices of control, negotiation, and influence that emerge from various actors within society. These actors can include government bodies, non-governmental organizations, civil society groups, private corporations, and even informal community networks. Cultural governance, in this sense, is a complex, multi-layered process that involves the interplay of legal frameworks, social norms, economic interests, and technological innovations (Qaissi, 2024). It is shaped by a variety of power dynamics, where different stakeholders vie for influence over cultural practices and the distribution of cultural resources. These dynamics may reflect broader societal values, political ideologies, and the shifting forces of globalization, with institutions such as museums, cultural foundations, and media networks playing key roles in mediating and reinforcing these power structures. The governance of culture often takes the form of formal regulations, such as intellectual property laws, copyright enforcement, and funding mechanisms, as well as informal practices like public opinion, media influence, and grass-roots advocacy.

Cultural policy, on the other hand, refers more specifically to the intentional strategies and programs deployed by public authorities to influence cultural production, participation, and access. It represents a more focused and often top-down approach, where government bodies design and implement policy frameworks aimed at achieving specific cultural goals. These goals might include the promotion of national identity, the preservation of cultural heritage, the fostering of creativity and innovation, or the expansion of cultural participation across social and demographic groups. Cultural policy can take various forms, including funding allocations, regulations, educational initiatives, and the creation of public cultural institutions. It is typically a product of governmental decisions, reflecting particular political agendas, economic priorities, and social values at a given time. In contrast to the more diffuse nature of cultural governance, cultural policy signals deliberate governmental action, often involving clear objectives and targeted interventions designed to direct cultural outcomes in a specific direction.

This chapter attempts to interrogate how emerging AI frameworks influence the conditions under which intercultural relations are produced, mediated, and governed in a digital context. As a result, the chapter approaches interculturality as not only a theoretical or ideological concern but also a *structural* and *policy* issue that must be addressed in the context of AI development. (For a further discussion on the notion of interculturality as a critical conception and praxis for probing into the organization and configuration of political authorities within cultural diversities in various contexts, see Qaissi, 2025.) It foregrounds the significant asymmetries between global centers of technological innovation—often characterized by wealthier, Western countries—and peripheral regions, which are frequently underrepresented in the design, regulation, and application of AI within cultural and creative sectors. Furthermore, it examines the role of governance in shaping more equitable intercultural futures, where diverse cultures can participate on equal footing in the digital age. In this context, the cultural governance of AI emerges as a critical site for reimagining interculturality—not merely as an abstract concept involving dialogue or representation but as a tangible, material question that encompasses issues of access to technological resources, the infrastructure necessary to support cultural expression, and the fundamental right of communities to shape and control their own cultural narratives in the algorithmic age. Through this lens, the governance of AI in cultural sectors becomes a pivotal means by which to address inequalities and ensure that cultural diversity is preserved, nurtured, and promoted in a globalized, digitally mediated world.

8.2 AI, policymaking, and governance

The integration of AI into policy frameworks serves as a crucial barometer for understanding and assessing the evolving logics of governance mirroring these global technological progresses. A case in point is the aforementioned *Government AI Readiness Index* (Oxford Insights, 2024) which evaluates countries based on the three key pillars of government, technology sector, and data and infrastructure. These dimensions measure the existence of national AI strategies, the level of investment in AI research and development, the robustness of digital infrastructure, and the ethical and regulatory frameworks in place. Countries that rank highly in the index, such as the United States, the United Kingdom, and Canada, typically demonstrate strong institutional capacities, well-defined AI policies, and advanced digital ecosystems that facilitate innovation and public sector AI adoption.

The index highlights significant disparities in AI readiness across regions, reflecting broader digital divides and governance challenges. While high-income countries benefit from well-established AI ecosystems and regulatory frameworks, low- and middle-income countries often struggle with infrastructural gaps, limited investment, and underdeveloped policies for responsible AI implementation. The ranking also underscores the importance of ethical considerations in AI governance, particularly regarding data privacy, algorithmic bias, and public trust in automated decision-making.

A striking development in 2024 is the publication or announcement of 12 new national AI strategies—representing a threefold increase compared to 2023. More significantly, over half of these originate from low- and lower-middle-income economies, underscoring a growing engagement among nations historically positioned on the periphery of AI governance. Ethiopia, for instance, has become the second low-income country to formally release a national AI strategy, following Rwanda's precedent in 2023. Similarly, several lower-middle-income countries—including Ghana, Nigeria, Sri Lanka, Uzbekistan, and Zambia—have transitioned from conceptual deliberation to policy codification, solidifying their AI frameworks after initial developments in the previous year.

This trend is further corroborated by the *Global AI Index* (Tortoise Media, 2024), which lists four non-Western nations—China, Singapore, South Korea, and India—among the top ten AI leaders. The *Global AI Index* is a comprehensive benchmarking tool that ranks countries based on their AI capabilities and potential for future growth. The index evaluates nations across several key pillars, including talent, infrastructure, research, development, and government strategy, to provide a holistic view of their AI ecosystems. Countries like the United States, China, and the United Kingdom consistently rank at the top due to their strong research institutions and high levels of AI investment. The index also considers factors such as AI-related patents, startup activity, and the availability of skilled AI professionals, making it a valuable tool for understanding global AI competitiveness. One of the key insights from the Global AI Index is the widening gap between AI leaders and emerging economies. While developed countries continue to dominate AI research and commercialization, many low- and middle-income countries face barriers such as limited funding, weak AI governance frameworks, and insufficient talent pipelines.

Historically, neoliberal economic doctrines have championed deregulation and market liberalization, advocating for minimal state intervention to facilitate corporate expansion. The rise of AI technologies as a force in the global economy has prompted a reassessment of the relationship between state intervention and market self-regulation. Neoliberal economic theory fundamentally advocates for minimal state interference, arguing that market mechanisms are inherently self-regulating and more efficient in allocating resources (Friedman & Friedman, 2002; Jin, 2021). However, the reality of AI governance has exposed an inherent contradiction within neoliberalism: while the doctrine insists on economic deregulation, it simultaneously necessitates robust state structures that primarily safeguard corporate interests rather than engaging in direct economic management (Jin, 2021; McChesney, 2008). The increasing significance of AI in national and international competitiveness has compelled governments across the Global North and Global South to expand their roles in shaping AI ecosystems through financial investment, regulatory oversight, and strategic policy frameworks.

The notion of a self-regulating market, long championed by neoliberals, presupposes that innovation and technological progress emerge organically through competition and private sector initiative. However, the unprecedented nature of AI, characterized by rapid advancements, ethical dilemmas, and systemic risks, has necessitated significant state intervention. Contrary to neoliberal expectations, governments have actively engaged in AI policymaking to mitigate market failures, address social and economic disparities, and ensure national security in an era of algorithmic decision-making.

The paradox of neoliberalism is most evident in the way AI governance has evolved to necessitate a state-led approach. In both developed and emerging economies, governments have recognized the strategic importance of AI and have subsequently intensified their financial commitments and regulatory engagements. The EU, for instance, has implemented comprehensive AI regulatory policies aimed at invigorating ethical AI deployment while maintaining global competitiveness (Hylland & Primorac, 2023). Similarly, China's state-driven AI strategy, underpinned by substantial government investment and industrial policy, underscores the extent to which AI has become a domain of geopolitical contestation.

Beyond economic considerations, governmental engagement in AI policymaking is driven by broader societal imperatives. AI technologies carry profound implications for employment, privacy, and social equity, necessitating policy mechanisms that prioritize both economic growth and ethical governance. Nation-states are thus compelled to design regulatory frameworks that balance innovation with public accountability. This imperative extends to AI's role in media and cultural production, where state intervention becomes particularly significant. Unlike other economic sectors, media and cultural industries intersect directly with societal identity and daily life. The proliferation of AI-generated media and cultural content, therefore, demands strategic state policies that safeguard cultural diversity and public interest. This shift marks a resurgence of state influence in cultural policymaking, counteracting the unchecked marketization of AI-driven creative industries.

8.3 AI and the political economy of the creative and cultural industries

CCIs are increasingly recognized as key contributors to both economic growth and social development, making them a focal point for both market-driven and policy-driven strategies (Jin, 2021). From a market perspective, CCIs are valued for their potential to drive innovation, create employment, and stimulate economic dynamism (Valiati, 2025). These industries encompass a broad range of sectors—including media, design, fashion, film, music, and the performing arts—many of which have demonstrated strong resilience and adaptability in the face of economic disruptions. Their ability to generate intellectual property, attract investment, and facilitate cross-sectoral linkages positions them as strategic assets in contemporary economies.

Governments, on the other hand, often view CCIs as viable instruments for achieving sustainable development goals, particularly in areas such as cultural preservation, urban regeneration, and social cohesion (Belfiore et al., 2023; Bennett, 1998, 2013; Hadley & Belfiore, 2018; Jin, 2021; McGuigan, 2004, 2005). By investing in and subsiding cultural infrastructure, creative entrepreneurship, and cultural exchange, policymakers aim to leverage CCIs as catalysts for inclusive growth and community empowerment. These industries not only contribute to national identity and soft power but also play a crucial role in addressing social challenges, such as unemployment and social exclusion, by providing alternative pathways to economic participation.

The intersection of these two perspectives—market-driven economic growth and state-led development agendas—underscores the dual capacity of CCIs to generate both economic value and social innovation. Unlike traditional industries, CCIs operate within an ecosystem where economic objectives and cultural considerations are deeply intertwined. Their value extends beyond financial returns to include the promotion of creativity, cultural diversity, and social well-being. This dual function makes CCIs particularly relevant in knowledge-based economies, where intangible assets such as creativity, heritage, and intellectual capital are becoming increasingly significant drivers of competitiveness and sustainable progress.

Policy initiatives in this context, thus, would refer to an instrumentalist approach to CCIs that addresses wider, non-cultural policy concerns, such as job creation, economic growth, urban revitalization, or, as current trends suggest, social inclusion and community development (Qaissi, 2024). Crucially, what characterizes a cultural policy as instrumental is not solely the goals that the arts purportedly assist in achieving; rather, the instrumental aspect lies in emphasizing culture and cultural venture as a means, not an end in itself. As Vestheim (1994, p. 65) explains, instrumentality has its background in the ideology of decentralization, regionalization, and the local initiatives for which an infrastructure had been built up in the 1970s.

Clive Gray's (2006) notion of 'policy attachment', in particular, highlights a shifting focus on the utilitarian purposes of culture and, by extension, cultural policy. This enduring debate permeates the entire domain of cultural policy, raising critical questions about the 'appropriate' or 'optimal' forms of cultural policymaking. At its core, the discourse revolves around the dichotomy between cultural production and cultural consumption, and the subsequent priorities that arise: should resources be allocated to art education or to the maintenance of art galleries? What specific 'goods' should culture be mobilized to achieve? Sigrid Røyseng (2008) aptly characterizes this as the 'ritual logic' of cultural policy, wherein culture is imbued with an almost mystical capacity to enhance society—to make individuals and communities 'better' or to create more 'ideal' conditions. From Gray's perspective, this leads to the phenomenon of cultural attachment, wherein culture becomes subordinated to other policy imperatives, thereby diminishing its 'intrinsic' value. As such, culture is thus harnessed as a tool to address a spectrum of social issues that the state deems as priorities.

This growing insistence on arts and cultural policies to showcase benefits beyond the aesthetic has emerged as a significant trend within political and governing contexts across the board. The quest for alternative, if not superior, rationales for establishing cultural and artistic policies has resulted in an increasingly instrumental connection. The instrumentalization of arts and cultural policies entails distinct and specific outcomes for their implementation and underlying objectives. These outcomes, in turn, are linked to new modes of service and public culture provision which are distinct from traditional forms of provision as well as to new dynamics in the relationship between states and their citizens.

Another motive that can be observed within the framework of new AI technologies and governance is digital sovereignty. This refers to the concept that nations, communities, or individuals should have control over their own digital infrastructure, data, and technologies. This includes the ability to regulate and govern the digital space within their borders, ensuring that digital platforms, services, and data flows align with national laws, cultural values, and security needs (Srivastava & Bullock, 2024). Digital sovereignty seeks to address the growing influence of global tech companies and foreign governments over data and digital assets, advocating for policies that safeguard local control, privacy, and security. The importance of digital sovereignty becomes even more evident as the global expansion of AI sparks significant shifts across multiple economic sectors, although its integration into CCIs remains uneven (Jin, 2021). While governments in both the Global North and the Global South recognize AI's role in driving digital economies, they have largely deprioritized its potential within CCIs.

Such proliferation of AI in CCIs is intrinsically shaped by political and economic imperatives. Neoliberal digital economies tend to privilege corporate-led technological development, often marginalizing state-driven interventions in cultural production. AI's expansion has been marked by increasing monopolization, with dominant digital platforms exerting disproportionate influence over creative economies (Jin, 2021). These platforms dictate algorithmic visibility, revenue flows, and audience engagement, thereby reinforcing economic asymmetries that privilege large firms over independent creators and cultural workers.

The monopolization of AI-driven creative platforms by a handful of global corporations[2] presents a significant threat to the richness and vibrancy of intercultural exchange, as it systematically privileges content that aligns with dominant linguistic, aesthetic, and cultural norms. These powerful corporations, often based in the Global North, design and control platforms that determine the visibility and accessibility of cultural products, with their algorithms frequently favoring mainstream content that conforms to Western ideals of beauty, language, and storytelling. This results in a process of algorithmic standardization, where local and non-Western cultural expressions face significant challenges in gaining the same level of visibility, recognition, or support. Consequently, cultures that do not conform to these dominant paradigms are often sidelined, their creative outputs obscured, and their narratives diminished or misrepresented in the global digital space. In this context, interculturality goes beyond the mere symbolic recognition of diverse cultures; it becomes a matter of material access to the platforms that control cultural production, dissemination, and circulation in the digital age. For local and non-Western cultures, the lack of fair access to these platforms means they are deprived of the opportunity to shape their own digital futures, to engage in meaningful global cultural exchanges, or to assert their own identities in the face of powerful, homogenizing forces. A political economy that fails to actively safeguard cultural diversity within AI-driven platforms runs the risk of reinforcing entrenched cultural hierarchies, under the guise of promoting technological progress and innovation. In such a system, technological advancements are positioned as neutral or universally beneficial, when, in fact, they often mask deeper inequalities and contribute to the further marginalization of already vulnerable cultures.

Nevertheless, a counter-neoliberal approach to AI governance in cultural industries is emerging, characterized by state policies that actively foster AI-driven cultural production while prioritizing cultural diversity, intellectual property protections, and public sector involvement. This contrasts with market-driven AI applications that primarily serve profit-maximization motives. South Korea provides a compelling case of a state that has systematically embedded AI within its cultural policy framework, demonstrating an alternative model of AI governance in creative industries. Following the 2016 defeat of world champion Lee Sedol by AI system AlphaGo—a visceral demonstration of machine learning's disruptive potential—triggered South Korea's AI policy pivot, culminating in the Mid-to-Long-Term Master Plan (2016) and Data/AI Economy Promotion Plan (2019). It also culminated in the adoption of a unique public-private model where chaebols like Samsung and Kakao collaborate with government ministries. While these policies ambitiously targeted a 114% growth in Korea's data market (2018–2023) and establishing 100 big data centers, critics highlight contradictions in the 'private-led, government-supported' rhetoric—evidenced by the Presidential Committee on the Fourth Industrial Revolution's (PCFIR) top-heavy structure of 25 appointed elites (Jin, 2021). The plans prioritize industrial competitiveness through AI/big data convergence but reveal governance tensions: despite framing citizens as 'co-leaders' of an intelligent society, implementation remains ministry-driven, with 2019 reports showing Korean AI firms still lagging behind global peers like Google in scale (Jin, 2021). This reflects Korea's state-capitalist approach to AI, where national prestige projects often overshadow grassroots innovation or labor protections. Similarly, France has taken a proactive stance in regulating AI's impact on cultural sectors, particularly through its strong policies on digital sovereignty and the protection of European creative industries (Eclairion, 2024). The French government has implemented AI-driven initiatives to support independent filmmakers, music producers, and digital artists while ensuring that large tech firms comply with national regulatory frameworks.

8.4 AI, cultural policy and the development discourse

Development, as a concept, encompasses both an ongoing, intransitive process (*developing*) and a defined, transitive objective (*being developed*). This duality has led to a conflation of the process with the end goal in many discussions on development, where the dynamic trajectory and the static outcome are conceived as synonymous (De Beukelaer & Spence, 2018, p. 140). In the mid-20th century, as the term evolved to its current connotation, the objective of development became synonymous with achieving the 'modernity' associated with advanced industrialized nations. The process, then, was seen as the progression of economies, institutions, and populations toward the idealized state of these already 'developed' countries. However, the term 'development' is laden with historical complexities and remains a site of contestation, with ongoing debates concerning its definition, implementation, and intended targets (De Beukelaer & Spence, 2018; Pieterse, 2010). Before exploring the specificities of 'human development', it is crucial to interrogate the broader implications and meanings of development.

Development, a term that has long been entrenched in both transitive and intransitive conceptualizations, presents tensions between its static and dynamic connotations. The transitive aspect, encapsulated by the notion of *being developed*, suggests a fixed endpoint, often equated with modernity as defined by neoliberal standard economics. In contrast, the intransitive dimension of *developing* implies an ongoing process, one that is theoretically unbounded and fluid, reflecting the continual evolution of economies, institutions, and societies.

The dichotomy between 'developed' and 'developing' countries, which has underpinned much of the post-war development debate, is increasingly scrutinized for its reductionist implications. The conventional metrics, such as Gross Domestic Product (GDP), used to delineate this binary are both arbitrary and inadequate (De Beukelaer, 2015; De Beukelaer & Spence, 2018). GDP, as developed by Simon Kuznets in the 1930s, was intended as a measure of economic activity, not as a holistic indicator of societal well-being (De Beukelaer & Spence, 2018, pp. 142–143). While GDP may provide a snapshot of economic performance, it fails to capture the broader dimensions of human welfare that are central to the concept of development.

Empirical data further underscores the evolving performance of Africa's creative economy. Between 2010 and 2022, the combined share of African countries in global creative goods exports showed significant improvement, increasing from 1.91% in 2010 to a peak of 3.71% in 2020, before settling at 3.02% in 2022 (UNCTADstat, 2023). This upward trend contrasts with the previous decade's modest figures, reflecting a more robust participation in global markets. However, imports have consistently surpassed exports, leading to a persistent negative trade balance. Van Graan, however, emphasizes the complexity of such economic activity, suggesting that economic success cannot be measured solely by export earnings or GDP. For instance, Nigeria's Nollywood film industry employs more people than the country's oil sector, although the latter generates significantly higher (De Beukelaer & Spence, 2018, p. 133). This disparity raises critical questions for policymakers: should priority be given to industries with high economic turnover but limited employment opportunities, or to sectors like Nollywood that offer widespread employment but generate comparatively modest income?

The discourse on development transcends simplistic economic metrics such as export earnings or employment statistics. The United Nations Development

Programme (UNDP) advocates for a broader conception of development, focusing on 'human development', which encompasses non-economic indicators such as health and education. While the UNDP's Human Development Index (HDI) offers a more comprehensive understanding of human well-being than GDP per capita, it still falls short in fully capturing the capabilities that underpin human development (De Beukelaer & Spence, 2018).

Arterial Network, a pan-African umbrella organization for arts and culture, operates within a complex political environment where it cannot afford to narrowly focus on arts and culture. To gain legitimacy and attract partnerships and funding, the network must align its work and initiatives with broader development goals. However, rather than adopting the development frameworks of its partners, Arterial Network has asserted its independence by articulating a more holistic definition of development:

> the ongoing generation and application of resources (financial, human, infrastructural and other) to create the optimal conditions (political, cultural, social, economic and other) in which human beings may enjoy the full range of human rights and freedoms enshrined in the Universal Declaration of Human Rights.
>
> (De Beukelaer & Spence, 2018, p. 134)

This definition underscores a broader, more inclusive understanding of development, one that integrates cultural, political, and social dimensions alongside economic considerations, thereby promoting a development model that is deeply intertwined with human rights and democratic values. The emphasis on the *conditions* in which individuals live is particularly linked to the concept of 'capabilities', a fundamental pillar of the liberal normative theory underpinning human development. At the heart of this theory is the work of Amartya Sen, who contends that development transcends mere economic utility—commonly proxied by disposable income—and instead resides in the enhancement of people's social, political, and economic freedoms (De Beukelaer & Spence, 2018; Sen, 1995, 1999, 2011). Sen explains that development should allow individuals to pursue a life 'they have reason to value' (Sen, 1995, p. 5), highlighting the importance of human rights and dignity. It is critical to note that Arterial Network's conception of 'development' is far more rights-focused than the conventional understanding of human development. The distinction is crucial: high levels of human development, as traditionally measured, do not inherently guarantee the protection of human rights. The cases of Libya and Tunisia prior to their 2011 revolutions are illustrative. Both countries topped the African HDI in 2010, yet this did not shield them from the upheaval that followed. The revolutions demonstrated that high HDI rankings—marked by economic growth, life expectancy, education, and healthcare—are insufficient in the absence of broader human rights and freedoms.

The increasing integration of AI into cultural industries complicates these existing tensions, introducing new dimensions to the cultural economy and its relationship with human development. While AI has transformed various economic sectors, its role in CCIs remains contested. Governments and policymakers have, for the most part, approached AI through a predominantly economic lens, prioritizing digital economies, automation, and data governance while overlooking its potential to reshape cultural production, accessibility, and equity. This oversight risks exacerbating existing inequalities in the cultural economy, particularly in regions like Africa, where the digital divide remains a structural barrier to participation in global creative markets.

These development dynamics carry significant intercultural implications that are crucial for understanding the broader impact of technology on society. When AI governance models, designed within particular socio-cultural frameworks, are imported wholesale into diverse cultural contexts, they risk overlooking or disregarding local creative traditions, values, and socio-cultural realities. Such an approach can inadvertently reinforce existing epistemic hierarchies, where the knowledge, practices, and perspectives of marginalized or non-Western cultures are subordinated to dominant global narratives, often perpetuating inequalities. In this regard, it becomes essential to support AI applications within the CCIs that are culturally grounded and context-specific. This approach ensures that technological advancements are not merely extensions of global power structures but contribute to more equitable, culturally diverse, and contextually relevant outcomes. Cultural policy, therefore, must evolve to address not only the economic imperatives of technological development but also the pressing challenge of cultivating inclusive and pluralistic infrastructures for cultural expression. Such infrastructures should be designed to ensure that local voices, traditions, and perspectives are not algorithmically sidelined or rendered invisible but are instead empowered and amplified within the digital age. In this sense, cultural policy should play a pivotal role in enhancing intercultural equity, encouraging the development of AI systems that reflect the diversity and richness of human cultures while promoting mutual understanding and respect in an increasingly globalized world.

8.5 Capabilities, capacity-building, and human development: rethinking policy and practice

Martha Nussbaum (2003, 2011, 2016) and Amartya Sen's (1995, 1999, 2011) *capability approach* offers a compelling alternative to the GDP-centric model by emphasizing the importance of expanding individuals' freedoms and choices. This approach, which underpins HDI developed by the UNDP, seeks to move beyond mere economic performance and instead focus on the conditions that enable people to lead meaningful lives. Nussbaum's articulation of a set of central human capabilities provides a normative framework for assessing development, one that is inherently more inclusive and attuned to the diversity of human aspirations. But despite these advancements in development theory, the distinction between 'capacities' and 'capabilities' remains underexplored, particularly in the context of the cultural economy. While capacity-building initiatives are frequently touted as key to upholding sectoral growth, they often fall short of addressing the deeper, more structural factors that limit individuals' capabilities (De Beukelaer, 2015; De Beukelaer & Spence, 2018). The cultural economy, as both a driver and a product of development, necessitates a focus not merely on enhancing capacities—such as skills and infrastructure—but on nurturing the capabilities that allow individuals and communities to shape their cultural environments meaningfully—an idea that will be further discussed in relation to the value-based approach to cultural management.

This distinction is critical when considering the role of culture in human development. The cultural economy is not merely a passive beneficiary of development but an active participant in shaping developmental trajectories. For instance, the establishment and maintenance of cultural institutions require not only the requisite infrastructure and financial support but also a conducive socio-political environment that empowers individuals to engage with and contribute to these institutions. Thus, the relationship between culture and development is reciprocal; each influences and is influenced by the other. While conventional development frameworks may prioritize capacity-building as a means to economic growth, a more holistic approach recognizes the importance of capabilities in achieving genuine human development. This shift from capacities to capabilities is essential not only for the flourishing of the cultural economy but also for ensuring that development is inclusive and reflective of the diverse aspirations of individuals and communities.

The enhancement of cultural capabilities is inherently intercultural, as it involves fostering an environment where diverse communities can not only access but also shape their cultural landscapes in ways that reflect their unique histories, values, and aspirations. This process requires a fundamental recognition of the inherent dignity and agency of these communities to define their cultural identities on their own terms, particularly in the face of increasingly homogenizing technological systems. These systems, often designed with a one-size-fits-all approach, have the potential to dilute or erase the richness of local traditions and values, promoting a narrow, often Western-centric perspective that can marginalize diverse cultural expressions. In light of this, an intercultural capabilities approach to AI in cultural policy would advocate for the creation of policies, platforms, and infrastructures that not only accommodate but actively empower a wide range of cultural actors to thrive in the digital age. Such an approach would resist the flattening effects of dominant AI models, which often attempt to universalize specific worldviews and experiences, disregarding the diversity of human cultures. Instead, it would prioritize the development of AI systems and platforms that celebrate, amplify, and support the multiplicity of cultural expressions and practices across the globe, ensuring that no culture is left behind or forced to conform to a singular, predetermined standard. By placing emphasis on cultural empowerment and agency, this approach would help foster a more inclusive digital ecosystem where communities have the tools, resources, and autonomy to protect and evolve their cultural identities, thus contributing to a more balanced and diverse global cultural dialogue.

Martha Nussbaum's (2003) capabilities approach, which she describes as 'fundamental entitlements', provides a framework that outruns the abstract notions of human rights by translating them into more tangible, actionable forms. Nomi Dave elaborates on this by highlighting Nussbaum's distinction between Western conceptions of rights as *negative liberties*—where the state is required to refrain from interference—and *affirmative* or *positive* rights that obligate state action (Dave, 2015, p. 13). Nussbaum's articulation of the ten central human capabilities underscores the importance of these affirmative rights, offering a normative basis for policy interventions that aim to enhance human well-being.[3]

When contextualizing this approach within the context of cultural economy, the primary task is twofold: first, to identify the 'achieved functionings'—the specific outcomes that development policies should aim to realize through the enhancement of capabilities—and second, to determine the capacities required to achieve these outcomes. This process begins with an exploration of the freedoms and capabilities of individuals within CCIs and extends to broader societal contexts. The *Creative Economy Report* provides a valuable framework for this analysis, particularly in its discussion on the selection of indicators that can guide policy decisions (United Nations Educational, Scientific and Cultural Organization [UNESCO], 2013, pp. 128–131). Here, the emphasis on outcomes—be they economic, social, cultural, or environmental—demands careful deliberation about the objectives of focusing on cultural industries. This deliberative process is central to ensuring that the chosen path reflects the values and aspirations of the communities involved, aligning with Amartya Sen's notion of living a life we have reason to value.

Once policy objectives have been clearly defined in terms of capabilities, the next step is to assess the specific capacities required to achieve these objectives. Andy Pratt (2013) asserts that capacity building involves removing barriers to development through investments in skills, training, education, and infrastructure, thereby enabling industries to scale. While Pratt's argument is compelling, it necessitates a deeper inquiry into the nature of the capacities that need to be developed. He suggests that in many regions, the creative economy is relatively new, lacking a tradition of extended production. However, this perspective risks overlooking the historical and informal practices that have long existed within the cultural economy, even if they did not conform to contemporary terminologies like 'creative industries' (De Beukelaer, 2015). A capacity-building approach that neglects these existing practices may inadvertently perpetuate a modernization paradigm that fails to recognize the socio-economic realities on the ground. As Pratt notes, an entire range of support skills is essential for the functioning of creative processes and events. However, before identifying these skills, it is crucial to articulate the desired outcomes of the cultural industries—what they are intended to achieve—and subsequently, the activities required to realize these outcomes. This sequence underscores the importance of defining 'achieved functionings' as a precursor to determining capacity-building needs.

The integration of AI into cultural policy could therefore be evaluated through the lens of human development and capabilities, as outlined by Amartya Sen. If development is about enhancing the freedoms that individuals have to lead the lives they value, then AI's role in CCIs should not merely be measured by economic efficiency but also by its impact on cultural rights, creative freedoms, and equitable access to technology. The rise of generative AI in content creation raises ethical questions: Will AI-generated cultural products displace human creativity, or can it be leveraged to expand creative possibilities? Can AI democratize access to cultural production, or will it reinforce existing power structures where technological access determines cultural visibility? These concerns necessitate a policy response that ensures AI supports rather than undermines cultural rights and human capabilities.

The concept of digital sovereignty is crucial to this discussion. As AI becomes more embedded in global cultural infrastructures, questions arise about who controls cultural data, how algorithms shape creative visibility, and whether local cultures can assert autonomy over their digital ecosystems. Digital sovereignty, understood as the ability of nations and communities to govern their own digital infrastructures, offers a framework for protecting cultural diversity in an AI-driven world. Without policies that prioritize local content, ensure fair AI governance, and support creative industries in developing economies, the rapid expansion of AI could deepen the existing asymmetries between the Global North and the Global South in cultural production and distribution.

8.6 Conclusion

The integration of AI into the cultural policy landscape is not merely a technological development—it is a political and epistemological event that reshapes how culture is produced, valued, and governed. This chapter has sought to unpack the complex interplay between AI and cultural governance by situating these transformations within broader political-economic paradigms. In doing so, it has argued that the deployment of AI within the CCIs is shaped not only by economic interests but also by competing visions of development, state capacity, and the role of culture in society. As this chapter attempted to demonstrate, governments across the world are responding to AI in markedly different ways. While some, particularly in the Global North, emphasize innovation ecosystems and market competitiveness, others, especially in emerging economies, are attempting to align AI strategies with developmental goals such as education, inclusion, and cultural preservation. However, these national trajectories are embedded within global asymmetries that continue to structure access to technological infrastructure, epistemic legitimacy, and policy influence. AI is not neutral; its design, deployment, and regulation are inscribed with cultural values and power relations. As such, understanding AI's implications for cultural governance requires more than economic analysis—it demands an interrogation of whose cultures, whose values, and whose futures are being prioritized.

This brings us to the intercultural stakes of AI. While the term interculturality is often associated with dialogue, encounter, and mutual understanding, this chapter has approached it through the lens of governance and justice. AI systems, particularly those used in cultural production and distribution, operate within algorithmic architectures that are frequently biased toward dominant linguistic, aesthetic, and epistemological norms. From the marginalization of minority languages in recommendation systems to the concentration of visibility in global content platforms, AI risks deepening existing cultural hierarchies. In this context, interculturality is not a soft add-on but a critical demand: a call to embed cultural plurality, epistemic diversity, and equitable participation into the very foundations of AI governance.

Furthermore, the chapter has proposed reframing cultural policy through the capabilities approach, arguing that the goal of cultural governance in the AI era should be to enhance individuals' and communities' freedoms to shape, express, and sustain their cultural lives. This goes beyond capacity-building in a narrow technical sense. It requires policies that prioritize cultural rights, support diverse creative ecosystems, and resist the depoliticizing tendencies of market-driven technological development. In this regard, digital sovereignty and human development are not abstract ideals but necessary frameworks for rethinking how cultural futures are negotiated. As such, the *intercultural chrysalis* imagined in this volume invites us to confront these intersecting challenges. Rather than accepting AI's integration into cultural sectors as inevitable or neutral, this chapter has proposed a critical and future-facing agenda: one that centers human capabilities, prioritizes epistemic justice, and foregrounds the governance of culture as a key site in shaping pluralistic and equitable digital futures.

Notes

1 In his book, *AI for Critical Interculturality*, world-renowned interculturalist Fred Dervin (2025) puts forward the idea that AI can be engaged not just as a technical tool but as a critical partner in the study and practice of intercultural communication and education. Rather than viewing AI as a threat to human creativity or understanding, the book argues for its potential to reveal ideological biases, challenge dominant norms, and promote deeper reflexivity in how interculturality is conceptualized, taught, and researched. It positions AI as a kind of critical interlocutor—a reflective

mirror that helps uncover personal and systemic blind spots, interrogate knowledge production, and disrupt linguistic and cultural assumptions. The book combines theory, case studies, and interactive exercises to encourage a non-utilitarian, ethical partnership with AI, ultimately aiming to reshape the future of intercultural studies through a more critical and collaborative lens.

2 Examples of these include Google, Meta, OpenAI, and ByteDance.

3 In her list of central human capabilities, Nussbaum includes life; bodily health; bodily integrity; senses, imagination, and thought; emotions; practical reason; affiliation; other species; play; and control over one's environment, both political and material (Nussbaum, 2003, pp. 41–42).

References

Belfiore, E., Hadley, S., Heidelberg, B. M., & Rosenstein, C. (2023). Cultural democracy, cultural equity, and cultural policy: Perspectives from the UK and USA. *The Journal of Arts Management, Law, and Society*, *53*(3), 157–168. https://doi.org/10.1080/10632921.2023.2223537

Bennett, T. (1998). Culture and policy—Acting on the social. *International Journal of Cultural Policy*, *4*(2), 271–289. https://doi.org/10.1080/10286639809358076

Bennett, T. (2013). *The birth of the Museum: History, theory, politics*. Taylor & Francis.

Bullock, J. B., Chen, Y.-C., Himmelreich, J., Hudson, V. M., Korinek, A., Young, M. M., & Zhang, B. (2024). *The Oxford handbook of AI governance*. Oxford University Press.

Dave, N. (2015). Music and the myth of universality: Sounding human rights and capabilities. *Journal of Human Rights Practice*, *7*(1), 1–17. https://doi.org/10.1093/jhuman/huu025

De Beukelaer, C. (2015). *Developing cultural industries: Learning from the palimpsest of practice*. European Cultural Foundation.

De Beukelaer, C., & Spence, K.-M. (2018). *Global cultural economy*. Taylor & Francis.

Dervin, F. (2025). *AI for critical interculturality*. Taylor & Francis.

Devlin, H. (2019, April 12). Hospital develops AI to identify patients likely to skip appointments. *The Guardian*. https://www.theguardian.com/society/2019/apr/12/hospital-develops-ai-to-identify-patients-likely-to-skip-appointments

Eclairion. (2024, March 26). *IA, our ambition for France*. https://eclairion.com/en/ia-our-ambition-for-france/

European Monitor of Industrial Ecosystems. (2020). *Estonian public services in the age of Artificial Intelligence | European Monitor of Industrial Ecosystems*. European Monitor of Industrial Ecosystems. https://monitor-industrial-ecosystems.ec.europa.eu/news/estonian-public-services-age-artificial-intelligence

European Union AI Act. (2024). *EU Artificial Intelligence Act | Up-to-date developments and analyses of the EU AI Act*. https://artificialintelligenceact.eu/

Friedman, M., & Friedman, R. D. (2002). *Capitalism and freedom*. University of Chicago Press.

Gray, C. (2006). Managing the unmanageable: The politics of cultural planning. *Public Policy and Administration*, *21*(2), 101–113. https://doi.org/10.1177/095207670602100208

Grynbaum, M. M., & Mac, R. (2023, December 27). The Times sues OpenAI and Microsoft over A.I. use of copyrighted work. *The New York Times*. https://www.nytimes.com/2023/12/27/business/media/new-york-times-open-ai-microsoft-lawsuit.html

Hadley, S., & Belfiore, E. (2018). Cultural democracy and cultural policy. *Cultural Trends*, *27*(3), 218–223. https://doi.org/10.1080/09548963.2018.1474009

Heaven, W. D. (2020). *Predictive policing algorithms are racist. They need to be dismantled.* MIT Technology Review. https://www.technologyreview.com/2020/07/17/1005396/predictive-policing-algorithms-racist-dismantled-machine-learning-bias-criminal-justice/

Hylland, O. M., & Primorac, J. (Eds.). (2023). *Digital transformation and cultural policies in Europe*. Routledge. https://doi.org/10.4324/9781003334576

Jin, D. Y. (2021). *Artificial intelligence in cultural production: Critical perspectives on digital platforms*. Taylor & Francis.

McChesney, R. W. (2008). *The political economy of media: Enduring issues, emerging dilemmas*. NYU Press.

McGuigan, J. (2004). *Rethinking cultural policy*. Open University.

McGuigan, J. (2005). Neo-liberalism, culture and policy. *International Journal of Cultural Policy*. https://doi.org/10.1080/10286630500411168

Nussbaum, M. (2003). Capabilities as fundamental entitlements: Sen and social justice. *Feminist Economics*, *9*(2–3), 33–59. https://doi.org/10.1080/1354570022000077926

Nussbaum, M. C. (2011). *Creating capabilities: The human development approach*. Harvard University Press.

Nussbaum, M. C. (2016). Introduction: Aspiration and the capabilities list. *Journal of Human Development and Capabilities*, *17*(3), 301–308. https://doi.org/10.1080/19452829.2016.1200789

Oxford Insights. (2024). *2024 Government AI Readiness Index*. https://oxfordinsights.com/ai-readiness/ai-readiness-index/

Pieterse, J. N. (2010). *Development theory*. SAGE.

Pratt, A. C. (2013). *Promoting sustainable development through culture: Current status, challenges and prospects*. (Korean national commission for UNESCO, Ed.). Korean national commission for UNESCO. http://www.unesco.or.kr/upload/data_center/2013_Culture_and_development_Forum.pdf

Qaissi, A. (2024). Reframing cultural governance: Instrumentality and the discursive turn in cultural policy. *Journal of Public Policy and Administration*, *8*(2), 44–60. https://doi.org/10.11648/j.jppa.20240802.11

Qaissi, A. (2025). Ordering diversity, governing culture: The emergence of interculturality regimes. In H. R'boul (Ed.), *African-Decolonial interculturalities* (pp. 60–80). Routledge. https://doi.org/10.4324/9781003620204-6

Rankin, J. (2025, February 19). EU accused of leaving 'devastating' copyright loophole in AI Act. *The Guardian*. https://www.theguardian.com/technology/2025/feb/19/eu-accused-of-leaving-devastating-copyright-loophole-in-ai-act

Røyseng, S. (2008). *The Ritual Logic of Cultural Policy*. Fifth International Conference on Cultural Policy Research, Istanbul, Turkey. https://www.culturenet.cz/coKmv4d994Swax/uploads/2018/08/The-Ritual-Logic-of-Cultural-Policy.pdf

Screen Actors Guild-American Federation of Television and Radio Artists. (2024, May 7). *Keeping the workforce human in the age of A.I.* SAG-AFTRA. https://www.sagaftra.org/keeping-workforce-human-age-ai

Sen, A. (1995). *Inequality reexamined*. Harvard University Press.

Sen, A. (1999). *Development as freedom*. Oxford University Press.

Sen, A. (2011). *The idea of justice*. Harvard University Press.

Srivastava, S., & Bullock, J. (2024). *AI, global governance, and digital sovereignty* (arXiv:2410.17481; Version 1). arXiv. https://doi.org/10.48550/arXiv.2410.17481

Tortoise Media. (2024). *The Global Artificial Intelligence Index 2024*. https://www.tortoisemedia.com/2024/09/19/the-global-artificial-intelligence-index-2024

UNCTADstat. (2023). *Creative services exports of selected groups of economies (experimental)*. UNCTADstat. https://unctadstat.unctad.org/datacentre/dataviewer/US.CreativeServ_Group_E

United Nations Educational, Scientific and Cultural Organization. (2013). *Creative economy report, 2013, special edition: Widening local development pathways*. https://unesdoc.unesco.org/ark:/48223/pf0000224698

Valiati, L. (2025). *The political economy of the creative and cultural industries: Stitching perspectives for research, policy and practice*. Taylor & Francis.

Vestheim, G. (1994). Instrumental cultural policy in Scandinavian countries: A critical historical perspective. *The European Journal of Cultural Policy*, *1*(1), 57–71. https://doi.org/10.1080/10286639409357969

Acknowledgements

The following AI models were used in the volume for the creation of analytical data by some of the chapter authors:

Chapter 1: ChatGPT 4o and DeepSeek 1.1.8(70)
Chapter 2: ChatGPT 4o, 4.5, and DeepSeek 1.1.8(70)
Chapter 3: DeepSeek 1.1.8(70) and Kimi
Chapter 4: DeepSeek 1.1.8(70) and Gemini
Chapter 5: GPT 4o and 4.5

Index

Active participation 11, 117
Africa 12, 64–65, 74–75, 77, 81–82, 86–87, 97, 116
African philosophy 93
agency 4, 6, 8–9, 11, 23, 40–43, 45, 99, 117–118
AI as mirror 9, 43, 69
AI governance 2, 12, 56, 75–75, 78–81, 83, 85, 87, 108–109, 113, 116, 119–120
algorithm 3–4, 7–8, 11, 13, 17, 29, 42–44, 50, 63–64, 66, 68–70, 75, 78–81, 84–87, 105, 108–109, 112, 116, 119–120
anthropotechnical 2, 11
anxieties 2–3, 4–5, 7–8, 56
artificiality 12, 54, 56
authenticity 51, 56
axiological 57

bias 1–6, 8–11, 13, 19, 23–24, 26, 29, 31, 33–34, 39, 41–46, 51–57, 63–64, 67, 69–71, 78, 80, 84–85, 91, 93, 96, 101, 105, 108, 120

capability approach 116
capacity-building 116–120
coloniality 12, 56, 64
commodification 94–95
communitarianism 93
Compute North, South 85
concepts 2, 4, 11–12, 17–19, 22, 30–32, 35–36, 18–40, 42–43, 49–50, 52, 54, 56, 64, 69–70, 72, 75–78, 82, 85, 87, 95, 97, 99–101, 106–108, 111, 113–115, 119–120
consciousness 4, 8, 50, 75, 78
creative and cultural industries 13, 105, 110
creative entrepreneurship 110
criticality 23, 25, 46, 53–54, 64–65, 67–69, 71
cultural governance 106–107, 119–120
cultural infrastructure 110, 119
cultural nuances 12, 63, 67, 71
cultural policy 13, 105, 107, 110–111, 113, 116–117, 119–121
cultural representation 68
curiosity-driven interculturality 65–66, 71
curiosity-first interculturality 65

dehumanising 8
deterministic pessimism 1, 2, 8, 13, 24
development discourse 113
digital capitalism 43, 67
digital colonialism 29, 80

economic deregulation 109
economy 13, 38, 56, 91–96, 98, 106, 109–110, 112–114, 116–118
embeddedness 2, 53
english-medium instruction 18
epistemic injustice 18, 19–20, 23–25, 36, 69, 92, 101
epistemic presence 17
essence 12, 49–51, 98, 100
ethics 1, 7, 49, 56, 79–80, 83, 92, 96–97
existence 12, 18, 49–51, 77, 80–81, 83–86, 97, 100, 108
exploitation 1, 13, 19, 81, 84, 91, 93, 95, 97, 106

fairness 56, 75–77, 79–81, 84–86
fantasies 2, 9–11, 29, 31, 45–46
fear 1–10, 13, 31, 46, 70–71, 99

games ('Go', 'Mancala') 86
generative epistemic injustice 11, 19, 23
Global South 1, 41, 54–55, 64–66, 74, 86, 97, 106, 109, 112, 119
gobemouches 30, 33, 46
'guerrilla interlocutors' 11, 25, 47

harmony 38–39, 44, 75
hegemonies 3, 13, 40–42, 54–56, 64, 66, 69, 71, 91, 93
hermeneutical access injustice 11, 19–22
hermeneutical ignorance 11, 19–22
hermeneutical injustice 19
hermeneutical lacunae 69
homogenization 11, 17, 54, 112, 117
human complicity 12
human development 114–117, 119–120

ideologemes 30–32, 34, 38, 45–46
ideologies 3, 6, 8, 10, 18–20, 24, 26, 30–33, 38, 40, 43–46, 53, 57, 64, 107
imaginaries 11, 32, 45–46
inclusive feedback loops 70
inconsistencies 9
indigenous knowledge protection 70
individuals' lived experiences 7, 10–11, 21, 23, 25–26, 42, 68
institutional frameworks 106
instrumentality 92, 111
interculturologies 32
intergenerational learning 97

justice 1, 10–11, 17–25, 36, 41, 44, 47, 52, 54, 69, 75–80, 85, 87, 92–94, 97, 100–101, 120

knowledge production 11, 55–56, 91, 121

language barriers 41
local stewardship 71
localities 64–65, 68, 70–71

marginalisation 55, 77–78, 113, 120
marginalised communities 7
marginalised voices 10, 18–19, 43, 52, 65
messiness of the human condition 9
multilingual injustice 18

neoliberalism 6, 42–43, 74, 86, 92–93, 109, 112–114
neutrality 20–21, 24, 53
non-academic contributions to AI 70

Omoluabi 77–78
ontology 10, 12, 49–51, 98, 101
orientalism 64, 66
'otherwise' 2

personhood 12, 82, 92, 96–101
plurality 20, 54, 120
policy attachment 111
political economy 13, 38, 106, 110, 112, 119
polyloguegpt 70–72
power asymmetries 3, 56
privacy 79–81, 108, 110, 112

reflexivity 2, 4–5, 10, 12, 18, 25–26, 33, 36, 40, 43, 52–53, 120
regulations 75, 80, 106–107
relational personhood 12, 96
representation 6, 10, 19–20, 24, 54–56, 67–68, 86, 93, 107
resistance 21–22, 25–26, 44
restorative justice 97

scepticism 2, 6, 11, 42, 64, 66, 69, 78
self-awareness 4, 49–50
self-manipulating 33
Silicon Valley 74, 86
social robots 91
social roles 91–96, 98, 100
superiorist 82
surveillance 4, 10, 82
sustainable development 110

testimonial injustice 10–11, 19–21, 23
theory 1, 3, 10–13, 29, 32–33, 35, 41–42, 44, 51, 63–66, 70–71, 75, 77, 107, 109, 114–115, 117, 121
translation 2–3, 8, 29, 57, 63, 118

Ubuntu 12–13, 41, 77–78, 91, 93–101
un-learning 5, 18
uncertainties 4, 8, 46

value-based approach 117

well-being 41, 77–78, 82, 91, 110, 114–115, 118
Western-centric 6, 9–10, 13, 21, 32–33, 38, 40, 43, 45–46, 117

Yoruba 75, 77

For Product Safety Concerns and Information please contact our EU representative GPSR@taylorandfrancis.com Taylor & Francis Verlag GmbH, Kaufingerstraße 24, 80331 München, Germany

Printed and bound by CPI Group (UK) Ltd, Croydon, CR0 4YY
11/12/2025
02016971-0005